In the Storm

Fulfilling the Will of God

In the Storm

Fulfilling the Will of God

Dr. Ernestine C. Reems

Treasure House

An Imprint of

Destiny Image® Publishers, Inc.
P.O. Box 310
Shippensburg, PA 17257-0310

"For where your treasure is
there will your heart be also." Matthew 6:21

ISBN 1-56043-254-3

For Worldwide Distribution
Printed in the U.S.A.

Treasure House books are available through these fine distributors outside the United States:

Christian Growth, Inc.	Successful Christian Living
Jalan Kilang-Timor, Singapore 0315	Capetown, Rep. of South Africa
Omega Distributors	Vine Christian Centre
Ponsonby, Auckland, New Zealand	Mid Glamorgan, Wales, United Kingdom
Rhema Ministries Trading	WA Buchanan Company
Randburg, Rep. of South Africa	Geebung, Queensland, Australia
Salvation Book Centre	Word Alive
Petaling, Jaya, Malaysia	Niverville, Manitoba, Canada

Inside the U.S., call toll free to order:
1-800-722-6774
Or reach us on the Internet: **http://www.reapernet.com**

CONTENTS

PREFACE

Just as Jesus spoke peace to the churning waters of the storm, God speaks peace to our hearts when we are in tune with His will. In this book, I hope that you, the reader, will also discover that there is a safe harbor in which to ride out the storm. There is refuge, a place of solitude and peace. As you read this book, I pray that your hope and strength will grow along with your understanding. The message I have to share with you is God's message of peace and deliverance from the storms. May you see the hand of God in your life more and more with each page you turn. And in the end, I pray that the storms you face will only have the power to draw you closer to the Lord and to the fulfillment of His purposes in the earth.

I am deeply grateful for many individuals who helped me with editing and publishing this book. I give special thanks to Evangelist Christine Liddell, Attorney Ekita L. Mitchell, and the staff at Treasure House and Destiny Image for assistance in writing this book. I also express my gratitude for the support of the Center of Hope Community Church family; E.C. Reems Women's International Ministries; my husband, Paul Ewing Reems; my sons, Brondon Paul and Brian Ernest Reems, and other family members who are so faithful to me in my ministry. This book is dedicated to the memory of my wonderful father and sidekick in ministry, Bishop E.E. Cleveland, my loving mother, Matilda Cleveland, and my dear sister and friend Lois Ruth Davis. To God be the Glory!

Ernestine Cleveland Reems

FOREWORD

When Ernestine Cleveland Reems was a young girl, she was often told, "God calls whom He wills to preach His message." As a five-year-old girl, Ernestine became filled with spiritual visions of bringing healing to hurting people. She saw crowds of people with broken lives and she dreamed of ministering to them in hospitals, prisons, homes, and wherever else there was need. Little did she know that God was preparing to call her to preach His message of peace to a dying world. In fact, young Ernestine probably would never have believed that a frail, sickly girl like herself would be chosen by God to speak a special message to the men and women of today's world.

In this book, you will discover that special message God planted within Pastor Reems' heart. Through the words in this book, Pastor Reems shares God's Word with thirsty men and women, some of whom, at this very moment, may be feeling stressed, regressed, and depressed to the point of utter despair. This book is intended to speak to you, right where you are. You don't have to get cleaned up or get your act together before reading this book. Pastor Reems tells it like it is, and by doing so, she brings God's amazing, life-changing peace to work in your life.

Christians are often referred to as "God's chosen vessels," for God fills us with His love, joy, and peace through Jesus

Christ. But the word *vessel* also has another meaning. A vessel is a ship, a carrier of precious cargo. God sees us as vessels, which can be filled with His glory and carry our precious cargo to the world—if we choose to hold fast to our faith in Him through the worst storms of life. But often it is in these storms that we somehow lose our way, stumble, and become cast adrift from our moorings. These storms cause even the stoutest, most seasoned sailor to become struck with fear and cry for help. So where can we turn for deliverance?

I have known Pastor Reems for the past 30 years, and I was particularly honored that she asked me to write this foreword to her book. She has spread the gospel of Jesus Christ all across this country, from the West Coast to the East Coast, and from the North to the South. She has built up a ministry of women pastors who look to her for courage and leadership. She has been a mentor and an inspiration to me, and she has counseled thousands of women who were facing difficult storms in their lives. I know that God is using Pastor Reems to spread His message to a world that is desperately seeking Him.

As the founder of the E.C. Reems Women's International Ministries, Pastor Reems is a visionary. She preaches a holistic message about salvation for the whole person. Her ministry is particularly geared toward women and children, especially low-income women who might feel they don't deserve God's love. None of us are ever good enough to *deserve* God's love, but the beauty of God's love is that He loves us anyway. God's love is unconditional.

This book, *In the Storm: Fulfilling the Will of God*, is about storms. The book tells of three men of God who had to weather some fierce storms, including Jesus, God's only Son. Pastor Reems describes the biblical account of these storms and uses them to bring light to the storms of today—drug abuse, violence, family strife, and broken friendships. Through Pastor Reems' eyes, we learn that these storms are nothing new. Pastor Reems reveals even more to us about weathering these storms—through our faith and absolute assurance that God will deliver each one of us. Together, we can learn to go through the storms in our lives with our hand in God's steady, unflinching hand of peace.

The great evangelist Billy Graham once wrote, "Men desperately want peace, but the peace of God is not absence from tension or turmoil, but peace in the midst of tension and turmoil." [1] This is the kind of peace that Pastor Reems describes in this book. Not only that, she also shows us that God has a plan for us to have peace in our lives in the midst of these storms.

Pastor Ernestine Cleveland Reems certainly knows about storms, as she tells us in this magnificent book. But she also knows the Storm-Tamer. May your faith in Jesus Christ and your love of God grow with every page you read. This book will show you that God is with you, even in the midst of the storms.

As you read this book, let God's message of peace fall into the empty crevices of your heart. Let God fill you to overflowing with praise and submission to His will. Then let your light so shine before men so that all who see you will see the hand of God in your life. You, too, can be filled with the peace of God which surpasses, and calms, all storms.

Evangelist Christine Liddell
Center of Hope Community Church
Oakland, California
January 1, 1996

---

1.   *How to Be Born Again* (Waco, TX: Word Books, 1977), p. 23.

PART 1

REBELLION

CHAPTER ONE

JONAH: FULFILLING THE WILL OF GOD

Fire, and hail; snow, and vapour; stormy wind fulfilling His Word... (Psalm 148:8).

Why do we fear stormy weather? Is it because of the awful fury and devastating destruction contained within the fists of a storm? Or is it because storms force us to come vividly face-to-face with the awesome presence and power of God? When you're in the midst of a storm that God sends into your life, there is no escape.

Storms have swept this planet from almost the beginning, often bringing the devastation and destruction of uncontrolled lightning, wind, and water—including the very water and nitrogen that every living thing needs to survive. But it wasn't always this way. When God created the earth, He separated the waters in heaven from the waters of the earth and called the dry land forth from the seas (see Gen. 1:6-10). God created a world of perfect harmony, a paradise for us to dwell in and live without storms.

However, there came a fateful day when the very prized creations of God, Adam and Eve, hid themselves from God's presence because of their disobedience to God's Word (Gen. 3:8). Although they hid from God, He still searched for them as

He walked in the Garden of Eden because they were His chosen creations, and precious beyond compare in His eyes. As He looked for those whom He had ordained in His image, God called out to Adam, *"Where art thou?"* God still searches for Christians who are in hiding from His Word today. Sometimes He must create a storm just to get our attention.

Storms are nothing new; they just take many forms in our lives. Farmers through the ages have raised their hands in praise to God when a longed-for storm broke a drought and renewed their crops. Other people have looked to the heavens and angrily shaken their fists at God as rivers rose to sweep away homes and livestock or as lightning triggered devastating forest and prairie fires. Perhaps the most violent storms occur on the sea, where men have so little power to find shelter from the storm's power and have so little need of its violent wind and fury.

We are living in days when there are suffering people everywhere. Adversity has lashed out violently, and no community or people has been left untouched. Adversity breaks down racial, social, and economic barriers.

God's Will Is to Save

We are living in stormy times. Your storm might be in the area of your finances, employment, health, emotions, or spiritual life. It is important that no matter when the storm occurs, where it appears, or what form it takes, you must make sure that your will is in the right position. The position of your will, determines the duration and intensity of the storm in your life.

Your will can only be in one of three positions. It can be in *rebellion*, *submission*, or *deliverance*—in translation into the will of God. These are the only possible choices. The sooner you make up your mind to surrender *your* will to *God's* will, your storm and the storms around you will cease.

Once a young farmer was told he might lose his hand due to an unfortunate accident that severed his wrist. The young man replied glumly, "You might as well cut off my whole arm." The doctor replied, "It is to save your life that we must cut off the hand." In his grief over losing his hand, this young man failed to focus on something more precious—life itself. We often react like that young man when we suffer disappointments or set-backs in our lives. We ask ourselves, "What's the use of going on?" And we fail to recognize what is most precious of all, eter-nal life.

It is the carefully-pruned vine that bears much fruit. Is it so surprising that the great storms that blow through our homes, our communities, our churches, seem at times to be so highly personal? Storms are personal when they are directed by God toward His people to get their attention. I am sure that there have been many personal storms in each of our lives which, if properly understood, worked to bring us into a right relation-ship with God. God is in the business of saving lives.

I wrote this book because I am keenly aware of the power and possibilities of the storms of life sent our way by the direc-tion and will of God. Does this mean that I believe that God de-liberately causes bad things to happen to us, i.e., bad things happening to good people? Not at all. God does not *cause* bad things to happen to us. *We*—you and I—*allow* bad things to happen to us when we are disobedient to the will of God.

This book tells a message about how to get into right rela-tionship with God. These chapters will take you through differ-ent storms, storms in which you or I could very easily find ourselves at any moment. This book will show you how storms can be avenues of deliverance. More importantly, this book will show you how storms can get your will in line with the will of God.

Storms Change Lives

The Bible records three storms that literally "fulfilled God's Word" in the lives of men in radically different circumstances. The first biblical storm arose in the life of Jonah, whose life of denial was radically transformed by God into a greater life of prophecy and promise. The second biblical storm, from the life of Paul, came so quietly and unexpectedly that Paul defied fear and the opinions of others to become a great preacher in Rome as he continued in the will of God. The third biblical storm, from the life of Jesus, teaches us that perfect submission leads to perfect peace. Each of the storms in the lives of these three men shows us how we, too, can fulfill the will of God in the midst of the storm.

Fulfilling God's *Word* is a necessary step to fulfilling God's *will* for our lives. But first, you and I must be completely surrendered to God's *wisdom*. For it is not through our frail human knowledge that we shall be saved. It is only through the holy, wonder-working power of God that you and I can become instruments of His will.

The three biblical storms discussed in this book, although experienced by other men, still have the power to change you today! God wrought each of these storms to fulfill His purpose. Not one of these storms represents a blind act of nature, randomly occurring due to the physical properties of air and water. No, these storms were, and still are, *life-changing* storms— re-arranging storms, designed by God to radically alter the lives of people. These storms forever changed those exposed to the storm in such a way that they were thereafter instruments to the will of God. But, the most amazing thing about these storms is that each of them was so perfectly planned, pre-ordained, and orchestrated by God that they affected not just the people who directly experienced the storms, but the lives of many other people.

Jonah and the Storm

The first biblical storm, the storm of Jonah, arose in an unpredictable, unforgettable way.

Now the word of the Lord came unto Jonah the son of Amittai, saying, Arise, go to Nineveh, that great city, and cry against it; for their wickedness is come up before Me... (Jonah 1:1-2).

I am sad to admit that you and I could replace the word *Nineveh* with the word *America*, and it would still be true! The only reason this country is being spared from God's total destruction is because there are still a few people who know how to pray for this great nation. There are still some of you who have a desire to pray and the willingness to break the fall of rebellion. But, like many of us here in America, the people of Nineveh lived in luxury and plenty. They lived their lives only to satisfy their own desires, spoiled by the very wealth God had allowed them to possess. There was no room in their lives for prayer, and they certainly left no time for God. Does that sound familiar?

Wickedness doesn't begin in just one day. It starts as a seed planted in the soil; it quietly takes root in the hearts and souls of people and disguises itself in many shapes and forms. That seed grows as it is nurtured through the disobedience and selfishness in human hearts. Soon, one wicked seed will sprout an entire nation of overgrown weeds choking the very essence of the love of God out of the hearts of people and bringing waste to the land. Once a weed takes root, it becomes a very stubborn and difficult thing to remove.

Before the seeds of wickedness in Nineveh brought its total destruction, God spoke to the heart of a Jewish prophet and ordered him to prophesy to that foreign land.

Jonah Was Not Alone in the Storm

But the Lord sent out a great wind into the sea, and there was a mighty tempest in the sea, so that the ship was like to be broken (Jonah 1:4).

Often the devil is given credit for creating things that he had nothing to do with. The Bible says, "But the Lord sent out a great wind...." The Lord sent the stormy wind to get Jonah's attention. Jonah, however, was not alone in that ship. The stormy wind the Lord sent affected the other passengers on the ship as well. The spirit of rebellion is cruel. It not only affects who have yielded unto it, but it also affects those who come into its path. The Bible only acknowledges one person on the ship as being in rebellion, Jonah, yet all those on the ship were in the storm.

Storms are prevalent in our homes, schools, and communities. God is saying to His people, "*Come back to Me; you have left your first love.*" It takes time and effort to build a real relationship. It takes times and effort to build a real marriage. I visited one of my nieces in Houston, Texas, about four months after her wedding. During my visit, she pulled me to the side and said, "Pastor Reems, how was your marriage when you first got married?" I answered, "Well...." Then, I began to minister to this young woman, and explained to her that it takes about five years for a marriage to get established. Building a relationship takes time and effort.

In a natural marriage, the partners have to mature to the point that everything they have belongs to their spouse. Similarly, in our spiritual marriage, we are the Bride of Christ, and we must get to the place of total surrender where all we have belongs to Him. This is true love—*pure love*—for God, which keeps you attached to Him even while enduring the storm of your will.

It's Time to Wake Up

God is tired of us being drawn away of our own lusts. We have forsaken God; therefore, we are going down. Jonah knew that he had no business on that ship going away from Nineveh. He had the audacity not only to run from the assignment of God, but he also went down into the hold of the ship and went to sleep! When prayer was taken out of the schools, our educational system went to sleep. When prayer was taken out of our homes, our families went to sleep. When prayer was taken out of our communities, our neighborhoods went to sleep. And when prayer was taken out of our government, our nation went to sleep.

God uses storms in our lives to wake us up. Sometimes the storm takes the form of a funeral. Sometimes it's a natural disaster. Sometimes it's a crisis in our community. It will take some serious storms to bring us together. Pretty soon, there won't be *any* government assistance. For many people this will be a storm of crisis proportions; but if we would love our neighbor as we love ourselves, no one would go hungry. God is not allowing economic storm winds to blow for naught. We must wake up!

Denominational walls and strongholds must be torn down. The Church has been divided, and so the gates of hell have been triumphant. God has not called us to build miniature kingdoms on earth. Churches have become our own little kingdoms instead of places of power, deliverance, and restoration. We have been building Baptist kingdoms, Catholic kingdoms, Methodist kingdoms, and Pentecostal kingdoms while the real *Kingdom of God* has suffered violence.

We are all on assignment to be servants of God: We should be busy taking back what the enemy has stolen from us. Do you know that God is always willing to give us another chance to change? Not just a second chance (which is not enough for most of us), but *another chance* to become what He wants us to be. God is a God of love, and He loves us enough to want us to turn our lives around and be in His Will. Even when we mess up and don't get it right, if we are genuinely staying the course and depending upon His Word, He will deliver us from the wickedness of disobedience and sin so we can move back into His will. God has a job for each of us to do.

CHAPTER TWO

RUNNING AWAY: FEAR AND FLIGHT

You Have an Assignment

It seems as if the devil, who is the prince of the power of the air, has taken over America. Seldom can you turn on the television without seeing a story that evolves around some type of criminal activity.

The wicked shall be turned into hell, and all the nations that forget God (Psalm 9:17).

Each person who calls himself a part of the Body of believers has an assignment. America is only being spared by God because there are still a few people obeying the Word of God and endeavoring to complete their assignment.

Wickedness is not new in our day. It was also prevalent in the day of Jonah, and it did not escape God's notice.

Now the word of the Lord came unto Jonah the son of Amittai, saying, Arise, go to Nineveh, that great city, and cry against it; for their wickedness is come up before Me. But Jonah rose up to flee unto Tarshish from the presence of the Lord, and went down into Joppa; and he found a ship going to Tarshish: so he paid the fare

thereof, and went down into it, to go with them unto Tar-
shish from the presence of the Lord (Jonah 1:1-3).

The word of the Lord came unto Jonah, giving him an assignment to go to the great city of Nineveh and protest against
the wickedness and sin that was there. God has given many of
us in the local Body of Christ the assignment to cry loud and
spare not (see Is. 58:1).

After we are born again, many of us begin to look at sin dif-
ferently. We allow satan to persuade us into thinking that one
sin is greater than another. Our personal attitudes toward different kinds of sins cause us to classify or categorize them, as if to
say that God is only forgiving toward certain "kinds" of sins today. If the truth were to be told, many in the Body of Christ need
deliverance from many different sins, including the sin of having the "wrong attitude."

We have become like Jonah; we don't want to go into the
world and get our holy hands dirty in order to show someone
else the beautiful plan of salvation. *That's someone else's job,*
we think. *Let someone else do it.* But, what if there is no one
else to tell the wonderful story of Christ to the lonely person
you work with? What if there is no one else who will speak the
name of Jesus to the mailman on your block? By keeping silent,
we miss the plan and purpose of God for our own lives.

Nowhere to Run

When we walk away form the plan of God for our lives, we
are practicing open rebellion. We are running away. Jonah also
rebelled against God. He decided that he was going to abort the
plan of God for his life and follow his own plan. But first, he
had to run from God.

God gave Jonah a job to do, and this great man of faith and
power rose up, quickly skipped town, and headed in the opposite direction! Now we know that Jonah was a man of God. He
was a man who walked with God and talked with God. He was
a man who was close to God's heart because he was a man of

prayer. Jonah heard God's message. It just wasn't the message that he *wanted* to hear. It did not fit in with his plans for that day. He was a very busy man. Surely God could find someone else to preach to those heathens! Jonah was determined to try to escape from God's presence in his life. What he did not realize was that he could not escape from God's power.

Has God given you an assignment to do? Then what are you waiting for? Are you on the run to get the job done, or are you just on the run? You can try to run, like Jonah did, from God's presence. You can keep putting everything else ahead of God in your life. You can use all kinds of excuses about why you cannot get the job done that God wants you to do. Yes, you can spend your entire life on the run, but a confrontation is inevitable. You cannot run from God's power.

God uses people to confront sin. Oh yeah, I've heard those famous TV evangelist-types preaching on Sunday morning, and those people do not have a corner on the market of God's work. No, God uses just plain, everyday, working people to cry out against sin and to lead others to God. He wants His Church to rise up by the millions, instead of just one or two isolated prophets crying in the wilderness. God wants to hear a chorus of millions and billions proclaiming His name throughout all the earth. His people are the instruments through which He works His will.

Unfortunately, most of us like to follow in the footsteps of Jonah by running from responsibility. We run from responsibility in our daily lives. Husbands and wives rise up in anger against one another. Fathers leave their families; mothers neglect their children; children run away from their homes—all running away from each other. We are afraid to confront responsibility. We feel inadequate. We feel intolerant. We do not really believe we have the resources to cope. All these things cause us to run from ourselves, to run from each other, and to run from God. As long as we are trying to depend on our own will to see us through, we *are* inadequate, intolerant, and unable to cope.

God has all the strength we need and will provide it if we surrender our will to His will. When we give our lives to God, we can stop running.

It is easy to make excuses. In fact, it is too easy to blame everybody else for your position or imposition when the real source of the problem is a little "closer to home." When you keep on going down, you *need* something to shake you, wake you, and tell you to get up. God has a storm tailor-made for you!

We all need to begin dealing with God like we're going down! Sometimes, it takes a storm to loosen our grip on "self" and on all our favorite things. A stiff wind with some towering waves seems to override our petty gripes and selfish likes, and a good hurricane can quickly pull our eyes away from the TV set and focus our attention on truly important matters.

"But Sister Ernestine, I'm not going down." A lot of things keep getting worse and worse and worse, don't they? Do you know why? You are in a storm, and it is probably because you keep right on sinning! By running away from what you know God wants you to do, in your rebellion against God's plan for your life, you are running right into a storm!

The Storm Is Brewing

Jonah knew he had no business on that ship. God had told him to go to Nineveh, but we find him running away from God in the opposite direction. He actually thought he could cure his homegrown spiritual cancer of disobedience with a vacation cruise away from God. He believed the problem would solve itself if he moved to Tarshish (Tarsus), just like you may think your problems will solve themselves if only you could "move to Atlanta, Honolulu, Nashville, or even Hollywood."

The truth is that when you move, you pack up your spiritual baggage as well as your earthly baggage. If God calls you to preach repentance in some foreign place like Pickled Butte, Montana, or Bragadocious, Louisiana, but you run, then life won't be any different in Atlanta, Honolulu, Nashville, or even

Hollywood. Why? Because you are still in sin. "Just let me get to New York! I just know I can get a better job there, and I'll leave all this pressure behind me." Listen, when you and your baggage arrive in New York, your problems will have arrived too because you will still be in sin!

Jonah got on that ship going to "anywhere else but God's will," and then he had the audacity to go down into the hold and go to sleep! Some people disobey with defiance, but most people—especially Christians—disobey God through complacency and apathy. They're "asleep at the wheel." They look nervously over their shoulder, yawn, and then say, "This running business is tiring. I got away from that assignment, so now I'm just going to go to sleep."

Entire churches and communities are "asleep at the wheel" across America. They are on a collision course with their own neglect and aborted destiny, and they don't even sense the storm brewing overhead! This "sleeping sickness" is paralyzing every part of our lives and our society, from the work of the Church to the responsible maintenance of our freedoms as citizens of the United States! We expect people to call us and urge us to come to church. We snore the hours and days away while people bombard the media and pound on our doors in a failing attempt to get a sleepy, apathetic nation to vote for the best leadership. We only wake up long enough to gripe and complain about the "lousy elected officials" and say, "Somebody oughta do something about those guys!" Somebody "shoulda," and somebody "woulda," but nobody did—they were all asleep at the wheel of their own destiny!

Secular government often reflects the spiritual state of the people it serves. Given the terrible situation of our economy—with massive job layoffs, government corruption, and immoral laws being passed—it seems like we would be eager to vote—if we were awake. Do you see what God is doing? He is using the storm to bring us together.

If current "budget-balancing" trends continue, there won't be any more welfare programs left to be the "safety net" for the poor, the young, the elderly, or the jobless. That's going to bring us a little closer together; because God's Word tells me I will have to have to share my beans with you! If the government is broke, then as a Christian, I have to share my clothes with you, glory to God! The fact is, our bankrupt government is getting out of the welfare business. Is the Church ready for this? How about you?

It's Time to Come Together—God's Way

God wants His people to come together, but we have different ideas. We are so determined to pull apart from each other that we have built impregnable walls and towers around ourselves with the same passion and skill the workers used to build the Tower of Babel. We have segregated ourselves into spiritual ghettos and neighborhood territories, and some of us have carefully strung razor wire around our little church turfs to keep the heretics and sinners out. To the Lord, we must look like a bunch of children playing on His beach, trying to make our own private sand castles on our little strips of sand! He is not amused.

Ministers across this land are busy making kingdoms so they can sit like little kings on their own thrones over their own little domains, all "in the name of the Lord," of course. I've warned ministers time and again, "Don't just get in the pulpit with some powerful message that doesn't accomplish anything! You need to move these people out into their communities with the gospel! Don't fall into the trap of thinking you're better than your people while you lounge in your little office with your collar on backward!"

The ministers of the Lord are called to move the hearts of their people toward God. Then the people are to move their bodies, compassion, and resources toward the hurting people around them! That's the bottom line. As it is, our local churches are nothing more than a bunch of little kingdoms—the little

Catholic kingdom is on the south side, the little Methodist kingdom is over on the east side, the little Baptist kingdom is on the west side, and the little Pentecostal kingdom is on the wrong side of the tracks up on the north side. Each one of them has its own little "king" strutting around. The truth is that we're going down because we're neglecting, or running from, God's will! Unfortunately, we're taking our communities down with us!

The truth is that God did not call me and give me an assignment just so I could build my own little kingdom and "do it my way." I am nothing but a servant of the Most High on a mission to feed His sheep. I am not called to be some little queen or princess reigning it over my private religious kingdom; I'm just a servant under orders to feed God's people the Word of God and to love them. My goal is simple: I am called to feed and teach them so that they can learn how to develop their own relationship with God.

When Reverend Brother Jonah got on that ship to Tarshish, he quickly ducked below deck (just in case God was still looking), and he went to sleep in a place below his calling and destiny. The Church has taken its cue from a failed mentor. It has also fallen asleep in a place below its divine calling and destiny, and it seems to be deaf to the authentic voice of the Lord. Selfishness and stubborn disobedience has reduced the once glorious Body of Christ to a bunch of little cliques built upon the shaky foundations of the fear or adoration of man: "So you drive a Mercedes? O-o-h, that makes us best buddies. And you drive a Jaguar—how much did that cost you? Yeah, we're buddy-buddy too. And you drive a Rolls Royce? Then you are definitely my best buddy-buddy! What? You don't even have a car? Sorry, I don't have time to talk to you. I need to 'do lunch' with my buddies after the service."

Education is one of the newest building blocks for our walls of separation. "You've got a college degree and I don't. That means that you have to be stuck up and probably think you're better than I am, so I'm not gonna speak to you." The bottom line is that whatever you have, and whatever you are privileged to achieve, those things aren't really yours! Your life doesn't really belong to you anymore. The Word of God declares the truth, which we are judged by:

> *What? know ye not that your body is the temple of the Holy Ghost which is in you, which ye have of God, and ye are not your own? For ye are bought with a price: therefore glorify God in your body, and in your spirit, which are God's* (1 Corinthians 6:19-20).

Where Is Your Treasure?

The believers who are blessed enough to earn Ph.D.'s often leave the nest in which they were blessed and fly off to more profitable places. I don't believe that is the plan of God! Those anointed believers who receive special training or advanced degrees have gifts and training that their churches and communities need! They need to get busy in the Body and motivate others to shoot for the stars! Instead, they end up in Silicon Valley or migrate to New York City in an empty hunt for the bigger, better bucks. We should all remember the words of Jesus Christ:

> *For where your treasure is, there will your heart be also* (Matthew 6:21).

Many educated believers are busy trying to win the approval and fickle favor of hard-hearted business people, cynical investors, and double-talking socialites in a constant search for worldly success. You would be surprised to hear and see the things that are done on the other side of those doors. Those unredeemed people may be smiling and grinning to your face, but they talk about you when they get behind the door. They don't like you and they don't like me. They don't like any one in the Kingdom because of what we stand for. We need to reach them, but we don't need their approval to sanction our obedience to God! All too often, highly educated or gifted believers run from God's call and commission, and they pretend they're right.

They go to sleep in the hold of their ship bound for Tarshish. Meanwhile, God is riding in the storm that is about to capsize their dream boat!

In my opinion, the only reason to get an education is to come back to your community and help your people. "Yes, I got a Ph.D. Now, you only went to grammar school but you want to break out of the poverty cycle? Come on, brother. I'm going to fix you up and show you how to go through school. We're not going to stop until you've achieved the dream God put in your heart!" When we invest our gifts, our money, our education, and our talents into God's Kingdom, we will reap a rich harvest in both the natural and spiritual realms. However, there are no guarantees outside of God's will.

The enemy has contaminated our system and infected our attitudes with rebellion and selfishness to turn believers against one another. He has robbed us of our "family network" of support, encouragement, mentoring, and love. Thanks to the devil's maneuvering and our corporate love affair with the things of the world, we've lost our compassion and desire to reach out to the hurting. When we're not busy running from God to offer our bodies and energies to our "other" god, mammon, we keep ourselves busy judging and condemning others who "fall short" of our hypocritical standards.

Love Without Prejudice

I have counseled many young men and women who have fallen into the snare of homosexuality. They became homosexuals either through abuse or situations of extreme hardship that threw them into the company of practicing homosexuals. Many of them went out there into the world because they wanted to be "independent," which is usually just a politically-correct term for "rebellious." Finally, their "independent" ways and work habits (or those of their companions) caused them to reach a point where they didn't have anything to eat or any place to stay. When no one from the Kingdom offered to take them in, guess who showed up with open arms, plenty of food, and a spare bed? Homosexuals took them in, and then they put these young Jonahs on a guilt trip if they wouldn't let their hosts use their bodies. I've heard this story repeated by many of the homosexuals and lesbians I've counseled!

One woman told me, "Pastor Reems, I got into lesbianism because I had two children, no food, and no money to pay the rent. That woman came in and paid my rent. She bought us some food and helped me out. That's why I felt guilty. When she asked me to do what she wanted me to do, I felt like I had to do it. I never thought I'd become a lesbian." This kind of tragedy wouldn't happen if God's people were more sensitive and more willing to share with those in need. Instead, we hop on the nearest boat to Tarshish, and leave the hurting to seek help from the hurting.

Jonah's prejudiced opinions sentenced the people of Nineveh to hell, and his actions nearly executed the sentence! We need to quit judging people who are different or worse off than we. We don't know why they are in the position they are in. God has called us to embrace and love our enemies, not to judge and ridicule them.

One of the more popular "righteous judgments" ringing out from America's pulpits and at after-church lunch tables is, "Everybody who is on welfare is collecting our tax money because they are lazy. Tell the bums to get a job." The truth isn't that simple or open to judgment. Some people who are on welfare are trapped in a vicious circle as they dash from place to place trying to get jobs that still don't pay enough to house, feed, and clothe a family and provide childcare. Unfortunately, job applicants with no job skills or higher education get the short end of the stick when it comes to job opportunities and wage levels. In countless cases, these people just can't justify putting their children and family at risk by taking them off of welfare for a minimum-wage job that doesn't even cover their basic needs!

Lost in a Storm

For some reason, judgment and criticism come easier than mercy and encouragement—even for the redeemed! I was talking to a local business person in the courtyard of our church building when I saw a teenage girl—a pretty young girl—prostituting right in front of the church! I abruptly cut off my conversation with the businessman and confronted that girl. "Young lady, how dare you prostitute here! How could you dare to turn a trick here. God loves you, and I love you, but how dare you do this!"

That young girl looked at me and said, "Well, I know it's wrong, and I know I shouldn't be doing this. But I don't have anywhere to stay, and I don't have any food. I have nothing to eat!" Then she began to cry, and I knew she was telling me the truth. At that moment, the Spirit of God birthed a dream in my spirit. Right then I silently prayed, "God, I've got to get a place for girls like this young girl to live. I've got to help them!"

This girl was lost—in the middle of a storm—with no rock to grab onto, no stronghold to give her a foothold. Like Jonah and the men on Jonah's ship, we can so easily lose our way in the middle of a storm.

But the Lord sent out a great wind into the sea, and there was a mighty tempest in the sea, so that the ship was like to be broken. Then the mariners were afraid, and cried every man unto his god, and cast forth the wares that were in the ship into the sea, to lighten it of them. But Jonah was gone down into the sides of the ship; and he lay, and was fast asleep. So the shipmaster came to him, and said unto him, What meanest thou, O sleeper? arise, call upon thy God, if so be that God will think upon us, that we perish not (Jonah 1:4-6).

In the Church we spend most of our time asleep, and when we're awake, we spend too much time just talking. We talk about what should be done (but we never think about being the doers), or we chew up other people with prejudiced, judgmental gossip and slander. We need to get up and go on down to Nineveh! If we don't, then God will arise with a storm like He did with Jonah. I think God looked down on His wandering prophet and said, "I'll tell you what. I'm going to shake old Jonah up, even if I have to shake up everybody else on that ship too! I'm going to put them right at death's door. I can't have a man sleeping who should be preaching!"

CHAPTER THREE

GOD GETS JONAH'S ATTENTION

You may be in the middle of a bad storm right now, and you think you're going to die. Maybe you picked up this book because storms and trouble are the only things you think about nowadays. Listen: You aren't going to die before you fulfill your divine purpose—as long as you obey your Master. Yes, your ship is rocking because there is a storm raging in your life, but God is going to raise you up. He's telling you in your heart this moment: "I'm going to get you up. I'm going to get you out of this storm!"

And they said every one to his fellow, Come, and let us cast lots, that we may know for whose cause this evil is upon us. So they cast lots, and the lot fell upon Jonah. Then said they unto him, Tell us, we pray thee, for whose cause this evil is upon us, What is thine occupation? and whence comest thou? what is thy country? and of what people art thou? And he said unto them, I am an Hebrew; and I fear the Lord, the God of heaven, which hath made the sea and the dry land. Then were the men exceedingly afraid, and said unto him, Why hast thou done this? For the men knew that he fled from the presence of the Lord, because he had told them. Then said they unto him, What shall we do unto thee, that the sea may be calm unto us? for the sea wrought, and was tempestuous. And he said unto them, Take me up, and cast me forth into the sea; so shall the sea be calm unto you: for I know that for my sake this great tempest is upon you. Nevertheless the men rowed hard to bring it to the land; but they could not: for the sea wrought, and was tempestuous against them (Jonah 1:7-13).

The Chastening of the Lord

Human beings will go to unbelievable lengths to avoid dealing with hard problems! Most of us would rather try anything else than what we already know to do. The men on the ship with Jonah probably didn't need to cast lots because Scripture says the prophet had already told them he was running from God. The dice or bones they tossed seemed to point to Jonah as the culprit, but even after the prophet urged the sailors to throw him overboard, they went to the oars instead. It was a nice humanitarian gesture, but they were trying to escape a storm of the Lord's making! The prophet was fish bait because of his rebellion, and no wooden boat could keep him from his "fishing appointment."

Disobedience and rebellion will send you on a downward spiral. You cannot run from the assignment that God has given to you no matter how hard you try. God is omnipresent and omniscient (all present and all knowing). Jonah thought that he could jump on a ship and get away from his assignment.

Jonah had the same demonic spirit of rebellion that is present in the earth today. People are rebelling against God. Since rebellion is only a sin, a sin of the will, the terrible conditions in our communities today can all be explained: Sin is contagious. All the conditions and situations in our individual communities today are a result of various sins. We, as people, always want to play "the blame game"; blaming this group, that race of people, the government, or even God. Like Jonah, we fail to identify sin. It is not an economic problem. It is not a racial problem. It is not a discrimination problem. It is a *sin* problem. Jonah did not want to go to Nineveh to confront the sin issue because it would cause him to have to deal with the areas of sin in his own life.

Jonah, under the direction of his own will, was on a ship headed for Tarshish. The Lord sent out a storm to get Jonah's attention. Many times we complain about our storms but we fail to realize that storms can do great things in our lives. Storms can shake us until we get shaken back into the will of God. God only chastens those whom He loves (Heb. 12:6). He only allows storms to come into our lives for one purpose. He uses those storms to fulfill the word that He has already spoken over our lives.

God Wants to Wake You Up

Jonah had developed a type of religious spirit. He thought, like many of us think today, *I'll go to church; I'll sing in the choir; I'll pay my tithes; as long as I can keep this one little sin, rebellion. I don't have to go to Nineveh if I do everything else.* God had patience with Jonah. God knew that Jonah would eventually be going to Nineveh. But because of rebellion and disobedience, he went to Nineveh by way of the storm. Many times God puts you through a storm to get your attention. That is all that the storm is about. It is about redirecting your attention to the timing, plan, and purpose of God for your life.

We are asleep, and we are just mouthing empty words without putting any action behind what we say. I'm sure that Jonah talked about "those people" in Nineveh. I'm sure he talked about the homosexuals. He must have also talked about those who were on a lower social rung than himself.

It bothers me how we are quick to see the "flaws" in others, but we fail to recognize our own sin of rebellion against God. I mentioned earlier that Jonah was the only person on that ship who was in rebellion, but all who were on the ship were in the storm. God went to a great deal of trouble just to get Jonah's attention.

The Bible tells us that Jonah was asleep in the bottom of the boat in the middle of the storm. The devil would like to destroy many of us while we are in a lackadaisical state. Symbolically, Jonah represents the state of the Church today. The other passengers on the ship represent the world. The world is calling out to the Church for help, even as the other passengers called out to Jonah.

So the shipmaster came to him, and said unto him, What meanest thou, O sleeper? arise, call upon thy God, if so be that God will think upon us, that we perish not (Jonah 1:6).

The Church is asleep while the world is dying. The Church is in a deep sleep, snoring loudly, while the rest of the world is in agony. The people on that ship with Jonah were so desperate, that they waited for Jonah to tell them what to do, even if it meant calling upon his God, whom they did not believe in. Jonah told them that the sea would not be calm until they threw him overboard.

Throw It Overboard!

The Bible declares that even after they casted lots and the lot landed on Jonah, they still hesitated to throw him overboard. As long as Jonah was on that ship, the storm kept raging. Storms are raging in the lives of many people today because they refuse to throw the cause of the storm overboard. I can just picture everybody else on the deck trying to save the ship. Some were pouring out water. Some were throwing cargo overboard. Today, we also have some throwing out to do. Some of us need to throw sin overboard. Some of us need to throw habits overboard. Some of us need to throw relationships overboard, and some of us just need to throw our wills overboard.

The Bible instructs us in Second Corinthians 6:14 not to be unequally yoked, or in unequal relationships. We need to know why it appears that we are going down. If you're associating with down people, you can't help but go down. If you want to be used of God, you need to associate with people who are obeying the Word of God. The power of association is dangerous. Whatever you associate with will soon rub off on you. The people on that ship had to throw the yoke of rebellion overboard and disassociate themselves with Jonah in order for the storm to cease.

You and I need to make up our minds today that we will serve God wholeheartedly and throw sin and all of its various manifestations overboard. You and I have to determine that we are going with God all the way, no matter what the cost. After Jonah was thrown overboard and he was swallowed up into the belly of the whale, he purposed in his heart to obey God. When the whale regurgitated Jonah onto dry land, the Bible records that the Lord spoke to Jonah a second time concerning his assignment. The Bible declares that Nineveh was an exceedingly great city of three days journey (Jon. 3:3). This time Jonah did not hesitate, didn't take time to pack, didn't even blink. I can just see old Jonah running through Nineveh crying, "Repent, Repent." I can hear the people of Nineveh saying, "Why are you running?" Jonah probably replied, "I am running with the word of the Lord in my mouth. I can't stop, for God has already sent a storm my way to fulfill His word."

Today, many women, even Christian women, are in rapidly raging storms. The wind is blowing; the lightning is flashing; the boat is being tossed to and fro by the water. They feel that they need certain individuals in their lives and refuse to throw them overboard. It really bothers me to see women live in abusive situations. Time and again, these "female Jonahs" come into my office with tears streaming down their bruised faces. They sit in my office and tell me their husbands beat them, sell their TVs, jewelry, and cars to buy more booze or drugs; and then these men threaten the children when they're high. After they tell me about the "other women," or whatever, they ask me, "Pastor Reems, do you think the Lord wants me to stay there?" They don't need an answer from me—they already know what they should do. They just don't want to do it!

Like Jonah, these women made their beds below God's best for their lives. They married outside of God's will, and now everything is coming apart in the storm! It doesn't take much to counsel these women. I tell them, "I don't need to counsel you. I don't even want you to pray about this one—God's will is spelled out. If he doesn't get saved and allow God to change his bullying ways, then don't stay with him! How can you sit in an abusive situation and act like you just can't live without his 'love'? That's not love, that is abuse. Climb out of that storm and begin to trust and obey God. He will take care of you."

What really bothers me about Jonah and his modern-day followers is that the storm that is trying to get their attention is also endangering everybody else around them! And all they want to do is sleep! I just want to shout, "Jonah, wake up, why are you sleeping?" Our lost and dying world is crying out to the Church, "Help!" But the Church is busy snoring and snoozing on church pews. The only time the saints wake up is when they think someone might be trying to take their little position or title in the church hierarchy, while the lost are perishing outside the church walls!

Back to God's Basics

A lot of parents are facing terrible storms in their homes because they tried to raise their children every way but God's way. They did it Dr. Spock's way; they did it the humanist way; they even did it the way the TV sitcom people do it. Now their children won't even go to school, and they definitely won't go to college. There's a lot of anger in these children's hearts today. Our rebellion, as parents, has created a storm in their lives.

If you have young children, you need to teach them to love everybody. Don't teach them to be against anybody or anything except the devil. If you don't watch it and you pass along your own bitterness or prejudices, their anger may turn against you! Teach your children that they need to have an education. Teach them that they need to go to church. Instill in them the value of discipline early in life. With proper instructions from the Word of God, they could probably avoid some of the storms you have enountered.

If you know you're running from God, don't act like you don't know why you are in a storm! You're in that storm because you don't want to do things God's way! The only way out of the storm for you is to yield to God's will without excuses.

When Jonah disobeyed and rebelled against God, he went down. That is exactly where you and I go every time we disobey God! He may let us go in a different direction for a long time, but the storm of God always catches up to a "Jonah" just when he's fallen asleep thinking he has fooled God!

We may ignore God for a while, but when a funeral, a marriage crisis, a medical crisis, or a financial disaster comes along, we suddenly remember how to kneel down on our knees again! It's amazing how a crisis helps us recover our prayer skills. When God gets our attention, we suddenly decide we need to go to church and think that every problem will suddenly be solved. It doesn't work like that. When our rebellion triggers a storm, we just have to ride it out and let the storm take its course according to God's time. In Jonah's case, God arranged special accommodations to help Jonah concentrate on the really important matters of his life—without distraction.

Nevertheless the men rowed hard to bring it to the land; but they could not: for the sea wrought, and was tempestuous against them. Wherefore they cried unto the Lord, and said, We beseech Thee, O Lord, we beseech Thee, let us not perish for this man's life, and lay not upon us innocent blood: for Thou, O Lord, hast done as it pleased

Thee. So they took up Jonah, and cast him forth into the sea: and the sea ceased from her raging. Then the men feared the Lord exceedingly, and offered a sacrifice unto the Lord, and made vows. Now the Lord had prepared a great fish to swallow up Jonah. And Jonah was in the belly of the fish three days and three nights. Then Jonah prayed unto the Lord his God out of the fish's belly, and said, I cried by reason of mine affliction unto the Lord, and He heard me; out of the belly of hell cried I, and Thou heardest my voice. For Thou hadst cast me into the deep, in the midst of the seas; and the floods compassed me about: all Thy billows and Thy waves passed over me (Jonah 1:13–2:3).

We need to get back to the basics of our faith. We need that good old "shoutin' and stompin' " we used to do when we praised the Lord even though we didn't have anything but greens to eat! Too many of us have grown fat and content with the material things we have been blessed with. We have filled our houses with the gods of our success. We have run from God's calling to hide in our beautifully decorated homes and plush business offices.

We have buried our first love and passion for God under the shallow apathy of acquired intellect. We have become too sophisticated to show emotions over anything except our favorite sports teams or soap opera plots. Anything else reeks of "emotionalism and religious fanaticism." No, the fact is, anything other than obedience to God leads to rebellion, disobedience, and eventual death! God's storm will strip away every false god you are hiding behind. The only way out of the storm is to plunge into the raging waters of God's correction!

Yield to the Storm and Live

God grieves when He sees us keep going down. He is sending His storm into our lives and our churches because we have failed to raise up godly mentors and educators. We have preachers assembled around us who don't know how to preach. Even worse, many of our pulpits are filled with Jonahs who think they made it to Tarshish! They do know what to preach, but they are afraid of what men will think. Their rebellion has pulled their churches right into the storm with them! We need to hear the truth—whether it is convenient or not! Only the truth can set us free from our torment and from the raging waves of the storm! We need to yield to the truth and plunge into the heart of God where we will be healed and set free again.

I went down to the bottoms of the mountains; the earth with her bars was about me for ever: yet hast Thou brought up my life from corruption, O Lord my God. When my soul fainted within me I remembered the Lord: and my prayer came in unto Thee, into Thine holy temple. They that observe lying vanities forsake their own mercy. But I will sacrifice unto Thee with the voice of thanksgiving; I will pay that that I have vowed... (Jonah 2:6-9).

Jonah's only way out was to yield to the storm of God—to yield to the correction and reprimand of God. Once he plunged headlong into the will of God, then his destiny was once again firmly in the hands of God—even in the midst of the storm. Jonah's deliverance began the moment he told those sailors, "I tell you what. If you throw me overboard, then this storm will stop and you'll be okay. Get me off this ship because I'm to blame!"

We can learn two things from Jonah's confession. First, your healing begins with the first step of admitting your sin. Honestly recognize your sin and admit that you are running from the will and plan of God for your life. Second, if you are struggling with any unconfessed sin in your life, you need to "throw it overboard"! You need to discard whatever sin or rebellion is the source of the storm in your life. Just say, "I'm going to quit sitting around blaming everybody else for my situation! I'm going with God no matter what it costs." When Jonah went down in the belly of the whale, he remembered the Lord! He purposed in his heart to pay his vow and to keep his commitment to God. It is amazing what it takes to get our attention sometimes! We are blessed to serve a God who loves us enough and remains faithful to us even in the midst of our storms. Evidently He thinks we are worth it!

Repent and Be Restored

But I will sacrifice unto Thee with the voice of thanksgiving; I will pay that that I have vowed. Salvation is of the Lord. And the Lord spake unto the fish, and it vomited out Jonah upon the dry land. And the word of the Lord came unto Jonah the second time, saying, Arise, go unto Nineveh, that great city, and preach unto it the preaching that I bid thee. So Jonah arose, and went unto Nineveh, according to the word of the Lord... (Jonah 2:9–3:3).

Once you repent and commit, even while in the belly of your storm, you better prepare yourself for the miraculous. God will move Heaven and earth on behalf of an obedient servant. Once Jonah admitted his sin, repented of his disobedience, and renewed his commitment to God, he was instantly transported back into God's perfect will and destiny for his life.

I have to warn you; however, don't be surprised when God returns you to the same assignment that got you in the storm in the first place! Jonah was again handed the "Nineveh assignment": He was to evangelize the capital city of the very nation that was trying to conquer Israel and Judah! This time he obeyed. The Bible says it took Jonah only one day to evangelize a city that took three days to travel through.

If you're in a storm today because of disobedience, fear, or rebellion, then I want you to realize that God wants to deliver you right now. He only sends storms to get our attention and restore us to His place of blessing and anointing. God wants to make you whole today. God may be speaking to you about some things you need throw overboard. Don't hesitate once you know the Holy Spirit has spoken to do something. Don't rebel against God; because the storm of correction isn't pleasant. Obedience is much better than the sacrifice it takes to go through a storm!

This book was birthed after I personally endured some of the worst storms in my life! I had never been in situations that seemed so hopeless. One storm in particular went on for more than 18 months! I shocked my congregation by admitting to them that I had brought that storm upon myself. God allowed that storm to brew in my life to bring me to a place of humility, and it has changed my life and attitude forever.

I, too, was like Jonah. I rebelled against my assignment as a pastor. Yes, I was preaching, but at the same time I was also rebellious. Does that sound familiar? I was preaching and saying, "Lord, I'm just too tired to keep this up. I don't want to do this anymore. I want to do something else."

Rebellion can be as simple as refusing to do what God has called you to do. That was me, so God backed off and allowed a storm to blow into my life. It rocked my boat so hard that at one point, the enemy tried to get me to commit suicide. The devil, that father of lies, told me every day, "Give up. The people are not with you. They don't even like you! God doesn't like you either. In fact, nobody likes you." There were some nights when the devil whispered into my mind all night long. I couldn't sleep because he kept harassing me with his ugly words and accusations. The only reason you hold this book in your hands is because God covered me with His blood and lifted me up.

The end result of every storm that God sends into our lives is that God is glorified as His purpose is accomplished in the earth. Every time we obey God, He touches a multitude of lives—beginning with our own, but ultimately touching the lives of everyone with whom we are in contact. In every major move of God that has swept the earth, the salvation and restoration of many began with the obedience of one. Whether it was

Noah, Moses, Joshua, David, Ruth, Esther, Rahab, Isaiah, Mary, John the Baptist, Paul, or Jesus Christ, God began His work through one to touch many. God is speaking to you today. Obey, so that the many who desperately need the fruits of your obedience will be blessed!

PART 2

SUBMISSION

CHAPTER FOUR

PAUL: NO PLACE TO HIDE

The great prophet David has already told us that there is no hiding from the presence of the Lord:

> *Whither shall I go from Thy spirit? Or whither shall O flee from Thy presence? If I ascend up into heaven, Thou art there: if I make my bed in hell, behold, Thou art there. If I take the wings of the morning, and dwell in the uttermost parts of the sea; even there shall Thy hand lead me, and Thy right hand shall hold me* (Psalm 139:7-10).

The will of God is the only place in the world that is perfect and complete. However, this does not mean that whenever you are obeying God's will your life on this earth will always be calm and peaceful. Oh, no. Even while you are in the will of God, you can experience turbulence. You may actually experience some of the worst storms of your life while you are in the will of God, but God will help you to focus and find the rest you need in Him. I was on a plane flying out to minister in a certain city when the airplane began to experience turbulence. The Lord gave me peace on that plane. In the midst of that turbulence, He showed me the meaning of many storms in our lives. God showed me that in calm weather the pilots are often eating, drinking, and talking to one another while the aircraft runs on "auto pilot." "Auto pilot" is for when things are going good.

The flying is so smooth that you relax and take your eyes off of the main instruments. During a storm, however, the pilots must pay special attention to all the instruments on the panels to be sure that the airplane is going in the right direction.

Contrary Winds in the Will of God

Paul met contrary winds sailing from Sidon to Myra.

And when we had launched from thence, we sailed under Cyprus, because the winds were contrary (Acts 27:4).

Paul was in the will of God facing contrary winds. Contrary winds are winds that just seem to be hell-bent on blowing you in the wrong direction. The contrary winds can be accusation. The contrary winds can be hatred and jealousy. No matter what kind of wind it was, we know that it was contrary to the purpose of the ship. The wind pushed against the ship. Those contrary winds made it very difficult to sail to Rome. It was such a harsh wind that the Bible declares that the boat sailed slowly for many days.

Right now, turbulent winds may be blowing in your life. They may even be contrary winds. Contrary winds get your attention. It is very easy to fall asleep when everything seems perfect. It is easy to lose your focus when everything is going well. It is easy to become lukewarm in calm settings. When you're in the will of God, the Lord will use storms to keep you focused. You may say, "Pastor Reems, I believe that I am in the will of God. I am earnestly seeking Him in everything that I do. So why are these strong turbulent winds still blowing in my life?"

Paul was in a storm even though he was in the will of God. Now, God intended to use Paul in Rome, and God had already spoken to Paul even though Paul was in bondage. Paul was placed on a ship to be delivered to Rome as a prisoner of King Agrippa (Acts 27:10). Paul was in bonds, yet he counted himself not to be a prisoner of any man but a prisoner of the Lord (Eph. 4:1). His will was in submission to the will of God—even in bondage. We expect that when we are in the will of God everything will be "sugar and spice and everything nice." But, you can be still in the will of God and be in a real hurricane.

> *And when it was determined that we should sail into Italy, they delivered Paul and certain other prisoners unto one named Julius, a centurion of Augustus' band. And entering into the ship of Adramyttium, we launched, meaning to sail by the coasts of Asia, one Aristarchus, a Macedonian of Thessalonica, being with us ... And when we had launched from thence, we sailed under Cypress, because the winds were contrary* (Acts 27:1-2,4).

In this passage of Scripture, the wind is representative of the Holy Spirit. The storm represents the day of the Lord. It is easier to get through stormy situations when you understand their purpose. God uses storms to get your attention and perform His work in your life. But remember, satan also uses storms. The purpose of satan's storms is to make you lose sight of Jesus Christ to get you out of the will of God. Even though God allows storms to come while you are in His will to manifest Himself in your life, satan will take advantage of the situation to try to distract you.

The Storm in Obedience

Soon after this, Paul was in one of the worst storms of his life, but Paul stayed in the boat. When storms come, many people get out of the boat, but the boat represents the Word of God. It is also symbolic of the Church. Paul, the great apostle of the New Testament Church, stood on the swaying deck of an Alexandrian ship as a deadly storm raged around him, a storm that threatened to sink the ship with all 276 souls aboard. Why was this apostle being guarded by Roman soldiers and a centurion aboard a boat bound for Rome? And what was he doing in a storm like this? Had Paul disobeyed God? Was Paul really just another Jonah?

You and I can quickly identify with the pain and uncertainty of Jonah's storm, but maybe something about Jonah's situation just didn't fit yours. You may be in the middle of a raging storm but no matter how much you search your heart, you can't find any rebellion that may have caused the storm in your life! Is it possible to have a storm raging in your life and still be in the will of God?

There are times when we feel the urge to get out of the boat of obedience. We need to realize that we're not the only ones hurting. You aren't the only one in the storm. Brother Paul was in a storm. He was a member of the Sanhedrin. He spoke seven different languages. Paul sat at the feet of Gamaliel, the greatest scholar of the Torah of that generation (other than Jesus Christ). This was Paul, a Roman citizen by blood and training. He had it all. And he gave it all up for the name of Jesus. Now he found himself in chains. He was on a ship that was going down in the sea, and all he had done to "deserve" it was obey God! Are you in the same situation today? There's hope! God is still in charge!

Are you sitting down? Has anyone ever told you that it is normal for obedient Christians to run into storms when they decide to step out in faith and obey God? It is true, but there is a big difference between the storms that come because of disobedience and those that come because of obedience and faith! Although the winds in your life may seem to be just as strong and the waves look just as high as those in the storm that swept through Jonah's life, their purpose and source are different! We've already examined the details of Jonah's disobedience and the storm God sent to regain his attention. What does Paul's experience say about storms in our lives?

> *But thou hast fully known my doctrine, manner of life, purpose, faith, longsuffering, charity, patience, persecutions, afflictions, which came unto me at Antioch, at Iconium, at Lystra; what persecutions I endured: but out of them all the Lord delivered me. Yea, and all that will*

live godly in Christ Jesus shall suffer persecution
(2 Timothy 3:10-12).

The wind and waves of Jonah's storm brought correction, reproof, and restoration to the plan of God. The fury of Paul's storm had nothing to do with correction or reproof. Paul was not disobedient to God or asleep in the hold trying to hide from Him. Paul had anticipated the Lord's assignment to Rome and had already made plans to go there.

And [Paul] *found a certain Jew named Aquila, born in Pontus, lately come from Italy, with his wife Priscilla; (because that Claudius had commanded all Jews to depart from Rome:) and came unto them* (Acts 18:2).

After these things were ended, Paul purposed in the spirit, when he had passed through Macedonia and Achaia, to go to Jerusalem, saying, After I have been there, I must also see Rome (Acts 19:21).

And the night following the Lord stood by him, and said, Be of good cheer, Paul: for as thou hast testified of Me in Jerusalem, so must thou bear witness also at Rome (Acts 23:11).

Your boat of obedience may be your church, your marriage, your relationship to your in-laws or co-workers, or your personal call into the ministry! In any case, once you settle it in your heart that your storm didn't come from disobedience, then keep your eyes on God and not the circumstances. Don't abandon ship unless God tells you to!

There were many times Paul could have given in to the storms in his life and ministry, but he didn't. Although he received 39 stripes five times, was beaten with rods three times, was stoned and raised up, was shipwrecked three times and floated adrift on the open sea for a day and night, and endured rejection, hunger, nakedness, and betrayal—Paul never gave up (2 Cor. 11:24-26). He relied on the Lord's strength, not his own.

I know that strong winds sometimes blow against your heart and mind, but rather than backslide or give up, stay in the boat! Some people backslide as soon as their confession of faith in some area leads them into a storm of opposition or trial. Don't be one of those people who quits the church as soon as something doesn't go your way. Look closely at Paul's journey in the storm. It might make the difference between your failure and your success! The bottom line is that all of us need the Church! We need to know that there is some place we can get in touch with God and be in the rich company of godly people!

God Provides Help in the Storm

And when it was determined that we should sail into Italy, they delivered Paul and certain other prisoners unto one named Julius, a centurion of Augustus' band. And entering into a ship of Adramyttium, we launched, meaning to sail by the coasts of Asia; one Aristarchus, a Macedonian of Thessalonica, being with us. And the next day we touched at Sidon. And Julius courteously entreated Paul, and gave him liberty to go unto his friends to refresh himself (Acts 27:1-3).

Any time you run into a storm because you chose God's way over your own, God will bless you. Paul was in a multitude of stormy winds. Paul was experiencing turbulence in the will of God, but God did not leave him alone; He gave him a confidant. I believe that Luke was on the ship with Paul because Luke wrote the Acts of the Apostles in the first person. Luke was a good friend to Brother Paul. He was not only a friend in good times but also in adverse situations. Many times in the church when people have these types of friends, others want to call them cliques. But when you are doing the work of the Lord, you need someone to walk with you. The Bible plainly tells us that another man named Aristarchus was with Paul too. Aristarchus was Paul's "companion in travel" (Acts 19:19), "fellow prisoner" (Col. 4:10), and "fellow laborer" (Philem. 1:24). He was dragged into a stadium because of Paul in Thessalonica (Acts 20:4). When you are in the will of God, He will provide for you and give you favor, even in the midst of the storm.

God even arranged for Paul's "jailer" to be a centurion who respected him and was extremely kind to him throughout his trip to Rome. They didn't really treat him like a prisoner at all. Early in the trip, before the storm hit, Julius the centurion basically told Paul, "I want you to go and meet with your friends" (Acts 28:3). This man may have been a Christian too, especially since he saved Paul's life when the Roman soldiers wanted to follow strict Roman law and kill all the prisoners aboard to prevent escape (Acts 17:42-43).

Paul was a prisoner at this time, but he was given the opportunity to go see his friends at Sidon, relax, and refresh himself. God provided refreshment for Paul while he was in captivity! By giving Paul favor with the guard, God was saying to Paul, "I know that you are a prisoner, but because you are *My* prisoner, going to do My will, I will prepare this table of refreshment for you in the presence of all your enemies."

There are no blessings that God will withhold from you. He will never leave or forsake you—even in the storms! I don't understand people who say, "Nobody wants to help me." For anything that God tells you to do, He will also give you someone to help you!

I've experienced all kind of storms over the last decade, but God always sends me some help. He is always out there looking for faithful people. At times, I wanted to jump off the ship God had put me on because I thought I might like something on some other ship. But each time, God has said, "You aren't going anywhere, Ernestine, except the place called 'there,' where I have called you to go."

No Easy Way

Many of you are on a journey to your place of destiny, your Rome, but right in the midst of it, you have run into a storm.

Don't be discouraged. When God speaks to us about a project or a dream He wants us to reach for, we often expect everything along the way to be "a bed of roses." We want every day along the way to be filled with sweetness, wonderful peace, joy, and glory. I must be blunt and warn you that sometimes you will all but lose your life in the will of God!

And when we had sailed slowly many days, and scarce were come over against Cnidus, the wind not suffering us, we sailed under Crete, over against Salmone; and, hardly passing it, came unto a place which is called The fair havens; nigh whereunto was the city of Lasea. Now when much time was spent, and when sailing was now dangerous, because the fast was now already past, Paul admonished them, and said unto them, Sirs, I perceive that this voyage will be with hurt and much damage, not only of the lading and ship, but also of our lives. Nevertheless the centurion believed the master and the owner of the ship, more than those things which were spoken by Paul (Acts 27:7-11).

Sometimes all hell breaks loose even when you are squarely in the will of God! Too many people come into the Church looking for an easy way out. Most of the time, it looks like we just want to shout and dance our way to Heaven. I'm sorry, but *that's not in my Bible.* If Paul is right, then once you commit yourself to Jesus, once you agree to offer your body as a living sacrifice to Him and as an instrument of righteousness, then a storm of persecution will come your way! If we call Jesus *Lord*, then we also have to accept the fact that we will have trials, hardships, and tribulations in this life. The good news is that God will always bring you through!

Things looked pretty bad for Paul. He was far from the lush surroundings of the Jewish religious elite he'd lived with most of his life. Now he was a prisoner under guard, and he sensed by the Spirit that the ship he was on was headed for disaster. Even worse, when he warned the ship captain and the Roman centurion, they didn't listen! My friend, if you haven't already learned the hard way, then be prepared to be ignored when you speak the Word of the Lord to others. These men probably thought, *Well, this Jewish fanatic is babbling again. He doesn't know anything about sailing or about the commanders in Rome—they're not interested in excuses! Why should we listen to him? What is his source for this ridiculous information?*

Paul tried to talk to the people, and he tried to reason with them, but in the end he was left with one hope against all others: God. Even when you are in the will of God, the storms generated by your enemies or the adversary will once again bring you to your true foundation—God. Either He has called and anointed you for His purposes or He has not. Americans live in a pampered bubble of ease and apathy that deprives them of the cutting-edge faith experienced by Christians in crisis and danger. We look up to missionaries who "put it all on the line" in foreign mission fields, but God is calling us to do the same wherever we live! The dynamic life of faith and obedience is incurably exciting. God is never so real as when you are in a storm and His hand is the only hand that can bring you out! Paul was in a deadly storm. His only means of escape was through the hand of the Lord.

Paul received a clear assignment from the Lord to go to Rome. Most of us get in trouble because we say "God said" when He didn't say anything. Then we bring shame on His name when it is clear we got into trouble through our own disobedience. Listen, if God tells you to do something, then He will take you through it. You may have to weather storms along the way. You may have to believe Him for finances or miracles along the way, but in the end you will make it because His Word is on the line.

CHAPTER FIVE

STORMY WINDS IN THE WILL OF GOD

Scripture teaches us, as the people of God, to "watch and pray" (Mk. 13:33). God does not intend for you to live in fear or anxiety. When you are watchful and sensitive to His voice in your spirit, you will know about approaching storms ahead of time. When possible, you can avoid them altogether. At other times, when your path takes you directly into and through a storm, you can stand fast in the security of knowing you have obeyed the Master and you are in His hands.

Caught Off Guard by a Storm

And when the south wind blew softly, supposing that they had obtained their purpose, loosing thence, they sailed close by Crete. But not long after there arose against it a tempestuous wind, called Euroclydon. And when the ship was caught, and could not bear up into the wind, we let her drive. And running under a certain island which is called Clauda, we had much work to come by the boat: which when they had taken up, they used helps, under-girding the ship; and, fearing lest they should fall into the quicksands, strake sail, and so were driven. And we being exceedingly tossed with a tempest, the next day they lightened the ship; and the third day we cast out with our own hands the tackling of the ship. And when neither sun nor

*stars in many days appeared, and no small tempest lay
on us, all hope that we should be saved was then taken
away* (Acts 27:13-20).

The Scripture says, "...and there arose..." Now that means
that they were sailing along exactly as they had planned and
everything was quiet and peaceful. The captain and the centurion
probably mentioned the beautiful sailing weather to one another,
saying, "See, old Paul was just having another religious vision.
We were right after all. Give me good old common sense every
time over this religious nonsense. We have schedules to keep,
orders to obey, and goods to deliver." Then, all of a sudden, a
storm arose. Now the seasoned sailors and the captain sailed the
Mediterranean Ocean and the Adriatic Sea for a living. They
had been trained to watch the weather and their lives depended
on their ability to predict weather patterns. They blew it this
time. This storm caught them off guard—in spite of the fact that
a prophet of God had warned them in advance, using the most
accurate weather forecasting system in the universe!

The storm that descended that day on Paul's life wasn't just
any old storm. It was a "Euroclydon" wind! This storm was as
violent as a typhoon with hurricane-like winds that beat and
battered the ship so hard that the sailors wrapped rope all the
way around the hull to keep it from breaking apart! This storm
didn't just "go away" after a quick burst of rain either—it lasted
about 14 days!

The name *Euroclydon* means "to billow from, or dashing
from the east." A *tempestuous wind* is one that is violent, ac-
companied by rain, hail, sleet or snow. When you get trapped in
the middle of turmoil, conflict, trouble, and pain, let me tell
you, it works on every area of your life! That is why I have so
much patience and love for the people of God. Sometimes the
enemy just beats on God's sheep from every side. Your finances
may be in ruins, your relationships may fall apart, you may even
lose your health, and all you can say is, "Oh, my Lord." You
might even be emotional like me and just go off somewhere to
scream. In my case, the Lord helps me right quick. He knows,

"Now this girl is about to lose her mind, so I think I'll help her a little sooner."

You need to know when the storm arises and recognize the source of the storm. If you are obeying the Lord, then the problem isn't with you. The storm is merely another obstacle to avoid or overcome as you obey God's will. Too many saints know Jesus, while not realizing or recognizing that there really is a satan who hates their Master and anyone who dares to obey Him. Thank God for the promise, "When the enemy shall come in like a flood, the Spirit of the Lord shall lift up a standard against him" (Is. 59:19b).

When the enemy comes in, you will quickly recognize it as the work of satan—if you are watchful and prayerful. The people on that cargo ship with Paul didn't know what was going on, but Paul wasn't worried. He knew God's Word and he knew satan. He couldn't be fooled.

God Keeps His Word

When God speaks to you, you have something to hang on to when the storms blow in your life. Paul was a free man when he entered Jerusalem to preach the gospel. He mentioned to his companions that he wanted to go on to Rome after he'd preached in Jerusalem (Acts 19:21). He figured there would be trouble, but he never planned to go to Rome as a prisoner! And he certainly didn't plan to die in the Mediterranean Ocean on his way to Rome!

However, everything seemed to blow up for Paul in Jerusalem. Paul's enemies lied about him to the Romans and tried to have him executed on the spot! He had to appeal to Caesar as a Roman citizen to save his own life! He ended up nearly winning King Agrippa to Jesus along the way, but he remained a prisoner. There was still a storm brewing that had his name on it! Nevertheless, Paul refused to give up or jump ship. He had a word from the Lord, and he wasn't going to back out!

One of the hardest things to find in the Church today is *fortitude*, an old fashioned word for an old fashioned virtue. Some people call it "stick-to-itiveness," but I just call it "having guts." You can't survive or ride out the kind of storm Paul went through by going to Sunday church services and maybe praying for 30 seconds before meals on Sunday! This kind of storm quickly separates the men from the boys, and the women from the girls. Only the strong in the Lord survive this kind of storm, and only the strong produce the kind of fruit and life-changing faith that Paul had.

Do you want to be a world-changer? Maybe you're like me. I have a lot of weaknesses and failures in my life, but I'm determined to follow the Lord—no matter what it costs. I know I can't do it in my own strength. Like Paul, I can only brag about my weaknesses, not my strengths. Paul boasted only in the Lord, never in his own abilities, education, or accomplishments.

No matter what storm is raging in your life at this moment, God is able and willing to bring you through. Whatever you do, don't try to make it in your own strength or wisdom. You'll just go down with the ship. Once you have settled it in your heart that your storm arose because you have dared to obey God, then take courage—God is with you! He won't abandon you to the wind and waves; He will lead the way.

Rejecting Godly Counsel Can Be Costly

Many times in our churches I see people who are in storms because they have not taken the time to listen to wise counsel. Paul had been counseled by God to admonish the boat's crew that there was a storm on the horizon.

> *...Paul admonished them, and said unto them, Sirs, I perceive that this voyage will be with hurt and much damage, not only of the lading and ship, but also of our lives. Nevertheless the centurion believed the master and the owner of the ship, more than those things which were spoken by Paul* (Acts 27:9-11).

Paul was misunderstood. Often in this Christian walk, we are misunderstood because in the natural world, things look good to everyone else, but in the spirit, a storm is on the way. The men who were sailing that ship were experienced seamen; whereas Paul was just a prisoner, a tentmaker, a former persecutor of the Jews. He did not bear the telltale marks of an experienced fisherman or sailor who had survived storms at sea. Because of pride and greed, they did not heed his words. They did not want to believe that this prisoner could tell that there would be a storm, a storm that they, the experienced seamen, could not see. Besides, the ship carried many valuable goods, which would fetch a pleasing price on the open markets. The seamen did not want to be stuck in Lasea during the winter, in a place where their goods had no value. They decided to reject Paul's advice and continue to sail full steam ahead.

It is just as important today that we submit ourselves and listen to those who have spiritual insight. One young woman in my church never made a major move unless she first came and counseled with me. I recall specifically one time when she was up for a promotion on her job that would result in an increase in her salary of over $20,000 per year. She came to me and said, "Pastor, pray that I am in the will of God." Although she had prepared herself mentally for the promotion and had all of the necessary skills and qualifications for the job, she still waited for the approval of the Lord. In doing so, she wisely sought the advice of godly counsel.

Years ago, this is how we lived. I recall that when I was a little girl, we would not dare make any move unless we first asked our pastor to pray for us and seek God's blessing for us in whatever it was we proposed to do. Somehow this generation has lost that kind of spiritual accountability to a higher spiritual authority. We live our lives as if they were ours to lead, and we fail to look to the true Leader, our God. Many are in storms today because they fail to recognize that there are hidden dangers along life's road, along the next path that they intend to take.

The storm ahead will cause them to lose many valuables along the way—just like the sailors on the ship with Paul. If those sailors had listened to godly counsel from Brother Paul, they would have made it to Rome with all their goods intact. If they had followed the advice of Paul, they would have had a couple of days delay, but they would not have had to go through the storm and lose everything.

Although Paul had advised against sailing because he knew that a storm was going to arise, he was in the storm nonetheless. If you are not careful in the storm, you can lose the most precious thing that you have. In the storm some have lost their peace. In the storm some have lost their joy. The sailors had to lighten their load. They had to give up some precious things just to stay alive in the storm. They had to free the ship from its burdensome cargo. They had to throw valuable merchandise overboard in the storm. They lost everything in the storm.

Don't be surprised when people ignore the things you have to say—even if your words are so anointed that they sizzle with God's presence! The centurion and the sea captain ignored Paul's prophetic warnings, and it nearly cost them their lives. They didn't know that Paul was speaking by the revelation of the Holy Spirit! Fortunately, they only made that mistake once!

Many local church congregations need to learn that although their pastor doesn't know everything about biology, psychology, medicine, or the latest designers, he probably hears from God. In certain situations, God will give a shepherd supernatural knowledge to bring deliverance, healing, correction, and encouragement to the sheep. If they reject their spiritual leader, they reject God's answer to their situation.

The person who knows God can have peace in the middle of the storm. The person who hears from God will also be able to hear God when He indicates the way out of the storm. The sailors on Paul's ship lost everything in the storm because they rejected God's message. Yet God still had a word for them through His servant who was with them.

CHAPTER SIX

SECURE AND AT PEACE IN THE STORM

Paul knew God. He told the men. "Be of good cheer, because last night an angel of the Lord came and spoke to me" (see Acts 17:22-23). When you are in the will of God in the storm, God keeps the lines of communication open. God never closed his ears to the prayers of His servant Paul. His ears are not closed unto the cry of His children. God sent an angel to comfort Paul in the midst of the tempestuous wind. The angel assured Paul that there would not be a loss of any lives on that ship.

Safe Within the Word

Now, Paul was on a ship with some very religious people. Paul was on a ship with men who had been fasting for 14 days, as was the custom. They had been fasting, but when the storm came, they wanted to jump overboard in order that they might swim to the shore. Some of them wanted to let down the anchor from the hold. To these religious men, Paul said, "You might as well eat, because you are religious. In your religious formalities, you have missed God." Paul told them, an angel of the Lord has said to me that all those who abide in the ship will be saved. We noted in Chapter Four that the ship represents the Word of God. If you stay in the Word of God and *stay with God*, you will be saved.

When Paul's captors set sail on the foolhardy hope of beating the winter weather, all he could do was trust in the Lord. Fortunately, God knows both the beginning and the end of every journey and every destiny. One young lady who grew up in my ministry learned valuable lessons about dependence on God and earnest prayer early in her career. She started out earning $30,000 a year. Then, through the guidance of the Holy Spirit, she started making $40,000 annually. She was up to a salary of $60,000 a year when she called me and said, "Pastor, I've prayed about this thing, and I think it is time to ask for $100,000 a year." I prayed about it, and then I told that young woman, "Girl, you go for it! Just go for it! You went to college, worked hard, and graduated with honors. Every time you have faced a challenge, you took it to the Lord. You were able to cope because you leaned on God. Now enjoy the fruit of your obedience and submission to God!" Life in the corporate world isn't easy for anybody in this world, but since that young woman put her life in God's hands, the sky has become the limit!

Authority in the Midst of the Storm

Brother Paul was under assignment, but the wind and waves of this incredible storm kept hitting the ship harder and harder. Things looked pretty grim the first day of the storm, but then they got worse!

When the storm hit, the sailors tried to plow directly into it, but the wind was too strong so they turned around and let the wind push the ship where it wanted. Finally, they saw a small island that seemed to break the force of the wind just enough to let the sailors strengthen the sides of the ship by wrapping ropes around its hull. Meanwhile the wind continued to blow, and they realized they could easily drift into the Syrtis banks, a treacherous whirlpool surrounded by sand bars off the coast of Africa. Desperate, the sailors pulled in what remained of the tattered sails and yielded completely to the force of the storm, hoping to run clear of the danger. The ship was totally out of control. And on the third day, after the men threw out all of their ropes and tackle to lighten the ship. When they threw the tackle overboard, they permanently lost their ability to effectively steer and sail the ship. They had given up any hope of surviving the storm. Then they were at the mercy of the storm's punishing wind and waves for 11 more days.

But after long abstinence Paul stood forth in the midst of them, and said, Sirs, ye should have hearkened unto me, and not have loosed from Crete, and to have gained this harm and loss. And now I exhort you to be of good cheer: for there shall be no loss of any man's life among you, but of the ship. For there stood by me this night the angel of God, whose I am, and whom I serve, Saying, Fear not, Paul; thou must be brought before Caesar: and, lo, God hath given thee all them that sail with thee. Wherefore, sirs, be of good cheer: for I believe God, that it shall be even as it was told me. Howbeit we must be cast upon a certain island (Acts 27:21-26).

I believe that angel came because Paul prayed for his captors! I'm sure Paul appreciated the encouragement himself, but God wanted to reveal Himself to the men on that ship with His apostle. The sailors still didn't believe Paul though. They secretly plotted to steal the ship's only lifeboat and leave the passengers, the soldiers, and the captain behind! They forgot one thing. There was a man aboard who heard from God! The Lord also gave Paul supernatural discernment so he could see this other danger:

And as the shipmen were about to flee out of the ship, when they had let down the boat into the sea, under colour as though they would have cast anchors out of the foreship, Paul said to the centurion and to the soldiers, Except these abide in the ship, ye cannot be saved. Then the soldiers cut off the ropes of the boat, and let her fall off (Acts 27:30-32).

The only way you're going to be safe in a storm is to keep your eyes on Jesus! You can be in the center of God's will and still be rocking in one of the worst storms you've ever experienced in your life. Keep your head up! You will be safe if you keep your heart and eyes focused on the Master of the storm! Don't listen to the devil—the storm isn't your fault! Storms may blow in from the jealousy of other Christians or from the pit of hell itself, but God is in control. You are a soldier with a mission from the Commander, and nothing but nothing can stop you if you have a heart to stand!

Brother Paul warned the centurion not to set sail in the stormy season. He had a word from God, but the Roman leader decided to trust in the words of man instead. The lives of the 276 men on that ship were at risk because of a human error in judgment, not Paul's failure or weakness. In fact, they were only saved because Paul was a genuine man of God with a mission that could not be stopped or hindered! Sometimes we get confused and expect God to provide for our material needs and guide us through storms of our own making!

We can't ask God to help us financially when we don't use wisdom with the finances that God has already blessed us with. We can't ask God to give us a powerful ministry in Africa or Europe when we won't witness to our neighbors next door. Don't bother to ask God for a leadership position in the church if you can't submit to your pastor or an elder in the local church! (I think we need to start praying for a little more common sense!)

God loves to bless and promote submitted and faithful servants. His delight is to lift up men and women who humble themselves under the Lord and under the leadership of their local churches. These people are mirror images of His Son, who submitted Himself to His Father in every way. Paul humbled himself before God and man. Even though he had every "degree" or rank you could earn in his day, he considered it all dung in comparison to following Jesus (Phil. 3:8). He knew how to honor God. I don't argue with people who tell me, "Pastor Reems, the Lord told me…": I believe that if the Lord tells you something, then He will bring it to pass! (Most of the time, He will bring it to pass along with some real storms.)

We all need to receive and obey our assignments, and we need to quit listening to the old serpent. He wants to cheat us and deceive us into thinking we are "out of the will of God" when we run into a storm or two. Something will happen to you in the will of God, but the Lord will make it work for good and not evil (Rom. 8:28)!

You may be like David and the apostle Paul! God may give you a highly visible position and then "set a table in the presence of your enemies" (Ps. 23:5)! God can show you things that your opponents are doing, and they just won't understand how you knew about their schemes. God may tell you what moves to make while your enemies scratch their heads and wonder, *How did he do that?* Trust in God, for He knows everything! God holds the top position in every corporation in the world. He holds the keys to our success in His hands.

There Is a Better Way

I'm deeply worried about the younger generation; they seem so stubborn and so sure that they know where they're going and what they should do. The fact is that all of us need to stop and listen more often. God may be speaking to you through someone you're trying to ignore! Had the centurion and the sea captain listened to Brother Paul, they might have made it to Rome with their ship and cargo in one piece and with much less worry! When you're going through a storm, if you're not careful, you'll lose something you shouldn't!

A lot of people want to sit around and blame everybody else because they're not where they think they ought to be! The real truth is that many times, *we're not where we ought to be because we wouldn't listen to anyone else!* Like most pastors, I'm amazed at some of God's children. I just look at some of them and say to God, "In some strange sort of way, I almost admire them for their determination." God is constantly trying to teach us things, but we're determined to do things our way. We don't mind going through the same storm, the same pain, and the same circumstances again and again! That takes a unique kind of fortitude. I love people who have determination, but I sure wish they would yield to God and let Him take them on to new places in His plan.

Have you ever wished you could wake up some of your friends and say, "Don't go that direction. Don't go through that storm, there is a better way! Just obey." That is what the apostle Paul tried to tell those men in the Book of Acts, but they were too impatient. They were discouraged over the slow progress they'd made in the first part of their voyage, so they let their attitudes cloud their judgment. Don't sit around and pamper discouragement. Don't feed and nurture a rebellious spirit.

More of us need to draw closer to God instead of depending so much on other people for guidance. Too many people in the church go through life without a real relationship with God, and they let other people direct their lives. Godly friends will point us back to God, but you don't need friends who point you away from what God tells you in His Word and in prayer. You don't need controlling people in your life. You need people in your life who say, "I'm going to pray with you about this thing. Come on, let's get the mind of God in this matter."

Prepare for Deliverance

Fourteen days passed from the day the storm hit until the day Paul stood up with a final word from the Lord about their survival in the tempest. The Bible says the crew and passengers had fasted for those 14 days, and Paul urged the men to eat and strengthen themselves for the final stage of their drama:

> *And while the day was coming on, Paul besought them all to take meat, saying, This day is the fourteenth day that ye have tarried and continued fasting, having taken nothing. Wherefore I pray you to take some meat: for this is for your health: for there shall not an hair fall from the*

head of any of you. And when he had thus spoken, he took bread, and gave thanks to God in presence of them all: and when he had broken it, he began to eat. Then were they all of good cheer, and they also took some meat. And we were in all in the ship two hundred three-score and sixteen souls. And when they had eaten enough, they lightened the ship, and cast out the wheat into the sea. And when it was day, they knew not the land: but they discovered a certain creek with a shore, into the which they were minded, if it were possible, to thrust in the ship. And when they had taken up the anchors, they committed themselves unto the sea, and loosed the rudder bands, and hoisted up the mainsail to the wind, and made toward shore. And falling into a place where two seas met, they ran the ship aground; and the forepart stuck fast, and remained unmoveable, but the hinder part was broken with the violence of the waves. And the soldiers' counsel was to kill the prisoners, lest any of them should swim out, and escape. But the centurion, willing to save Paul, kept them from their purpose; and commanded that they which could swim should cast themselves first into the sea, and get to land: And the rest, some on boards, and some on broken pieces of the ship. And so it came to pass, that they escaped all safe to land (Acts 27:33-44).

Brother Paul never wavered throughout that trip to Rome—even when the ship broke up in the sea, and the Roman soldiers wanted to kill all the prisoners to prevent an escape. (Roman soldiers paid with their own lives if a prisoner in their charge escaped.) Brother Paul didn't even flinch when a poisonous snake latched onto his hand when he was putting wood on a fire (Acts 28:3). He was on a mission from God, and nothing in Heaven, earth, or hell could stop him! That is confidence born out of relationship!

Some of us need to eat less and pray more. We need to fast from television and gaze on the face of the Lord who redeemed us. We're too busy getting "drive-up window," fast-food answers from everyone else. We need to put down those plates and pots, turn off that television, hang up the telephone, turn off the radio, and cry out, "Dear God, I have to hear Your voice! I'm hungry for Your presence, and nothing less will do!"

There are times in the storms of life when your body will be afflicted. Your heart will feel broken, and you may feel like your spirit is crushed. Your mind will be so confused that you can't find help anywhere. Praise God, you can reach out to the Lord! The writer of the Book of Hebrews wrote under the inspiration of the Holy Ghost:

> *Wherefore seeing we also are compassed about with so great a cloud of witnesses, let us lay aside every weight, and the sin which doth so easily beset us, and let us run with patience the race that is set before us* (Hebrews 12:1).

When you get in the midst of the storm, you need to wait on God. When you're in the will of God, the enemy brings the storm, hoping to draw, push, or knock you out of God's will. Many people allow satan's condemnation to separate them from God. As soon as they begin to feel uncomfortable because of the difficulty they're going through, they begin to think, *Well, maybe the Lord's not with me. Maybe the Lord didn't really say that.* But you need to stand and say, "I don't care what I have to go through, He still said it!" You fire right back at the devil, "God still said it. I lost my home, but God still said it and I'm going to do it! I lost my husband, but God still said it and I'm not going to quit!" Sometimes in a storm you lose the most precious thing you have. Some believers have been surprised when their whole family turned against them because of a storm.

When you get in a storm, the enemy will try to bring all kinds of adverse situations and roadblocks your way. Like Paul, you need to listen to the words of the Lord and stay in the ship until God says to abandon it. I don't care how the billows rage and how the winds blow. If the ship falls apart, glory to God! Stay in God's unchanging Word. If you stick with God's Word, then He'll bring you through. There is nothing He can't do. He is the Master of the wind and waves. No storm or weapon formed against you can prosper when you are dwelling under the shadow of the Almighty! You have His everlasting Word on it!

In righteousness shalt thou be established: thou shalt be far from oppression; for thou shalt not fear: and from terror; for it shall not come near thee. Behold, they shall surely gather together, but not by Me: whosoever shall gather together against thee shall fall for thy sake. Behold, I have created the smith that bloweth the coals in the fire, and that bringeth forth an instrument for his work; and I have created the waster to destroy. No weapon that is formed against thee shall prosper; and every tongue that shall rise against thee in judgment thou shalt condemn. This is the heritage of the servants of the Lord, and their righteousness is of Me, saith the Lord (Isaiah 54:14-17).

What did this man of God do in the face of impossible odds and opposition? Paul declared the Word of the Lord and took charge of the situation—even though he was a prisoner! How did he do it? He remained true to the vision and call of God, and the Lord took care of the rest.

Obedience Versus Disobedience

There are three unique patterns in Paul's storm that make it different from Jonah's storm of disobedience:

1. Paul's storm didn't "end" supernaturally. Paul survived supernaturally, and he also saved the lives of everyone who went through the storm with him. Jonah's storm could have been avoided altogether through obedience on his part. Paul's storm was due to no disobedience on his part.

2. Paul didn't jump from the storm to total safety. He was moved by God's Spirit from one plane of miraculous provision to another, giving God the glory at every step! Paul's storm was literally part of his mission and ministry on the earth, not just an obstacle in his path. Obedience and trust were part of Paul's daily lifestyle.

3. While the disobedience of others cost them dearly, Paul's obedience in faith and prayer preserved his life and those of his captors! The owner of the ship, who joined with the captain to convince the centurion that Paul's warning should be ignored, ended up losing his ship and his cargo. The captain and crew lost their jobs when the ship was destroyed. The soldiers could have lost their lives had any one of their prisoners escaped on the island of Malta (Melita). The centurion would have lost his rank and his life as well. But God had a plan, and He had a man who knew His voice.

God has a plan for your life and ministry today too! Does He also have a servant who knows and obeys His voice? If you obey Him, then that will make all the difference for you and for those who are in the storm with you! Take courage, my friend! Believe God, that it shall be even as it was told you (see Acts 27:26)!

There were many times when I wanted to jump out of the ship, but God was so good that he just loved me through my stupidity. The enemy makes it so easy for us to choose to go overboard. The enemy wants us to get out of the ship. The enemy wants us to get out of the will of God. Sure, satan is good at what he does. He even tempts those who are walking in the five-fold ministry callings. Sure, satan will make the grass look greener on the other side. He will give you an alternative to the Word and the will of God.

I recall a time when I went to visit a church for the purpose of evangelizing. The power of God was great in that place. The people said that they were going to invite me back again the next year for a bigger meeting. Immediately the enemy came to steal the purpose of God over my life for pastoring. The enemy spoke to my mind and said, "Maybe you should resign as pastor and go back into full-time evangelism. The people are asking for you to come back again." The enemy knows just what to bait us with and uses all the right words to trick us out of the plan God has for our lives. But, praise be to God, The Lord revealed *His* will for my life while I was in prayer about this decision. God said, "Hold onto the assignment that I have given to you, to preach to the people."

Seek God in Your Storm and Hold On

This is why prayer is important. When you know how to pray and get in touch with God, you always have a safety net. When you get in a real storm it will cause you to seek God. The story of Jacob always encourages me. Jacob said, "God, I am in a storm. I don't know what to do. You have been good to me, but Esau said that he was going to kill me. I have two wives and 12 sons. I need to hear from you. I am in a storm." Jacob decided to seek God in the midnight hour. The Bible declares that the Lord dispatched an angel and there he wrestled with Jacob and his hip was disjoined. (See Genesis 32:9-31.) Sometimes in the storm your body will be afflicted. Sometimes in the storm your spirit will be broken. Your mind might become confused or your heart crushed.

I looked in the Book of Hebrews during my storm of indecision. There a great crowd of witnesses is mentioned (Heb. 11–12). Jacob stepped forth as a witness. I can just hear him as he gave his testimony:

> "I was troubled on every side, yet not in distress. I was perplexed but not to the point of despair. I have been persecuted by my own brother but not forsaken; I have been cast down, but I haven't been destroyed. This time, Lord, I'm not going to let go until You bless my soul" (see Gen. 32:24; 2 Cor. 4:8-9).

Jacob was determined not to let the angel go until he got what he needed. This is how we need to be with the Word of

God in the storm. We need to be as adamant as Jacob was. Even with a disjointed hip, a divided family, and a crushed spirit, he was determined to hold on to the Word of God.

The Bible says that Paul had the same kind of determination, steadfastness, and singlemindedness of purpose. Although Paul's ship appeared to start to fall apart around him, he did not abandon ship. Paul kept his eyes on what was important, and he continued to pray. Prayer is what opens your eyes to that which you need to remember to hold onto. Sometimes it is only a piece of a Scripture, but you need to hold onto it. Don't worry if you don't remember the entire verse. Hold on to that Word of God. Don't worry about the words of your prayer and whether the words sound right. Just pray in sincerity and supplication. Those men on the ship with Paul didn't care what they were holding onto while the ship was being dashed and torn asunder. They grabbed whatever they could and floated ashore on broken pieces. *Broken pieces.* Sometimes all you have are the broken pieces of the Word of God, but hold on, because that is enough to keep you afloat.

I believe that Paul wrote some of the Scriptures while he was on that ship. Paul said that he learned to be content no matter what state he was in (Phil. 4:11-12). He learned to give thanks in all things. I can hear Paul saying, "I was in the will of God in the storm but I learned to be content. I learned to be both full and hungry. I learned to abound and to be without. I learned to float on the Word of God." Paul recognized that even in the will of God you can still be in the storm. While in the will of God you can lose everything, but as long as you hold to God's Word, you will always come out victorious. Paul learned that in submission, there is forewarning; in submission, there is blessing. Paul learned that in submission, there is confidence; in submission, there is a refreshing. Above all, he learned that in submission there is deliverance.

PART 3

DELIVERANCE

CHAPTER SEVEN

JESUS: FULFILLING GOD'S WILL

A storm is a serious disturbance of any element in nature. It is a sudden change in the balance of an atmosphere.[1] A storm is indicated by a violent commotion. When a situation is stormy, there is conflict, trouble, or turmoil. There are many types of storms. Some storms are sudden and come without warning.

The Bible tells us that Jesus was also in a storm:

And there arose a great storm of wind, and the waves beat into the ship, so that it was now full. And He was in the hinder part of the ship, asleep on a pillow: and they awake Him, and say unto Him, Master, carest Thou not that we perish? (Mark 4:37-38).

In the above Scripture, it says, "there arose a great storm of wind…." Before the storm arose, there was no sign of a storm on the horizon. The clouds did not begin to darken. The air did not begin to dampen. The sun did not go into hiding. The ship did not cast shadows on the water. All of a sudden, there was a

---

1. See *Merriam Webster's Collegiate Dictionary*, 10th edition (Springfield, MA: Merriam Webster, Inc., 1994), p. 1160, for a complete definition of *storm*.

full blowing storm. Instantly, there was a violent commotion in the atmosphere.

Don't Be Surprised by the Storm

A true believer should never be surprised by stormy weather. The Bible teaches us that we are to continue in prayer and watch (Col. 4:2). Prayer strengthens our spirits, keeps us in communion with God, and equips us to fight the devil. When you watch, you keep yourself constantly informed of the plans and tactics of the enemy. Being watchful means being alert. Being watchful helps us to recognize when the enemy is planning to send a storm our way. Many saints recognize the Lord, but do not recognize satan. The Bible tells us that even when the enemy would come in, the spirit of the Lord would act as a flood and wipe out all of his devices, if we are praying and watching (see Is. 59:19).

In Part 1 of this book, we talked about Jonah. Jonah was in disobedience to the will of God. He boarded a vessel to escape to avoid the will of God and found Himself in the worst storm he would ever face in his lifetime. Only his confession of guilt and submersion in the sea saved the men aboard that ship. His repentance in the belly of a fish put him back on track and allowed him to fulfill God's purpose.

In Part 2, we talked about the apostle Paul, whose obedience to God landed him in chains aboard a vessel of persecution bound for Rome. The 14-day storm that destroyed that ship threatened the lives of every man aboard. Paul's obedience and intercessory prayer saved them all, and allowed him to fulfill the purpose of God.

Now, there is a third man who faced a life-threatening storm in an entirely different way. Jesus faced a violent storm with His disciples, but not because He was disobedient. He was not simply *being* obedient to God's will either. Jesus *was* the will of God in the storm!

Jesus was the embodiment of the will of God. Before departing from the shore, Jesus prayed to the Father. Then He said to His disciples, "Let us go over unto the other side." Jesus was in constant communion with God. He knew that he would make it to the other side because God had already ordained specific lives on the other shore that Jesus would touch. Jesus was the Will of God walking in a flesh house. He was so in tune with the purpose of God that He could sleep in the storm. He knew that satan was going to cause havoc on the waters, but He was in tune with God's purpose. He knew that on the other side of the Lake of Galilee lives were waiting to be healed, delivered, and restored.

You Are Not Alone in the Storm

You can be right where God wants you to be and the devil will cause a storm to come your way to try to divert the plan of God. The enemy only comes to steal, kill, and destroy (Jn. 10:10). In the middle of the storm, he comes to steal your peace, kill your faith, and destroy the plan of God in your life. In the middle of the storm you cannot afford to become confused and run off and leave the Church, God, or His Word. We talked about Paul's storm and how those who kept a piece of the ship made it to safety. Stay in the Word. The Word of God teaches us in Psalm 23:4 that although we walk through places where everything has the appearance of death, we should fear no evil because God is with us.

> ...when the even was come, He [Jesus] saith unto them, Let us pass over unto the other side [of the Lake of Galilee]. And when they had sent away the multitude, they took Him even as He was in the ship. And there were also with Him other little ships. And there arose a great storm of wind, and the waves beat into the ship, so that it was now full (Mark 4:35-39).

Are you struggling with the wind and waves of a great storm in your life? Have you experienced a serious disturbance in your life? Have you ever felt the pressing weight and distress of "a violent commotion" in your life or family? Isn't it amazing to see how things can be going along so smoothly and quietly, when all of a sudden a storm will rise up to ravage our lives?

We need to rejoice over our moments of peace in this life. We need to be thankful for the times our lives are free of commotion and violent disturbances. Unfortunately, most of us "notice" peace most when it is gone, when it is suddenly displaced by a raging storm and by upheaval in every area of our lives. When a storm arises, everything seems to just erupt and go the wrong direction! A storm can arise in anyone's life. It can strike our physical well being, and it can attack our emotions. A storm can arise to cripple our finances, and sometimes, it may even seem to paralyze us spiritually!

> *And He* [Jesus] *was in the hinder part of the ship, asleep on a pillow: and they awake Him, and say unto Him, Master, carest Thou not that we perish?* (Mark 4:38).

Do you feel the battering winds and suffocating waves of a storm as you read these words? Are you weary of battling the force and fury of the storm sweeping over your life? I'm talking about the kind of storm that can make you feel confused, even though you "know that you know" that you are saved? Believe me, those violent storms can rattle you! One minute, you absolutely know that Jesus Christ is the Son of God and that you are abiding with Him. The next minute, you begin to question yourself, "Maybe He's not really…"

The storms that swept into the lives of Jonah, Paul, and even Jesus Christ, were all marked by continuous turmoil, conflict, and trouble. The storm that hit the disciples in the fourth chapter of the Gospel of Mark wasn't just a passing storm front or a quick tropical squall that would only last an hour. No, this was a persistent, deadly, and unpredictable storm with life-threatening intensity. The high wind whipped the waves so high that they washed over the sides of the ship, filling the hull with water faster than they could bail it out (Mk. 4:37). Of all the types of storms, this one, a sudden, intense storm, was the kind that all men feared. It took the storm of a lifetime to frighten professional fishermen like Peter, Andrew, James, and John! This was no ordinary storm; it was supernatural in its origin and vicious in its power.

God Is With You in the Most Destructive Storm

At least seven of the 12 disciples in the boat with Jesus were experienced commercial fishermen who had grown up fishing on the Lake of Galilee. They knew that lake very well, and they knew about its peculiar weather patterns. The Lake of Galilee is the world's lowest freshwater lake, with a surface some 680 feet below sea level and a maximum depth of 150 feet. Roughly 13 miles long and 7 miles wide, it has an area of 90 square miles.[2] Some of the snow-capped mountains beside the lake tower up to 2,000 feet above the water, while the climate at the water's edge is tropical. The difference in temperature creates violent winds that rush down the sheer canyons onto the lake with predictable results.

One researcher and author described the winds he encountered during his stay on the eastern shore of the Lake of Galilee:

"The sun had scarcely set when the wind began to rush down toward the lake, and it continued all night long with constantly increasing violence, so that when we reached the shore the next morning, the face of the lake was like a huge boiling caldron...We had to double-pin all the tent ropes, and frequently were obliged to stand with our whole weight upon them to keep [them]...from being carried off bodily into the air."[3]

---

2. George Cansdale, "Fishing in the Lake of Galilee," *Eerdman's Handbook to the Bible*, ed. David Alexander and Pat Alexander, (Grand Rapids, MI: William B. Eerdmans Publishing Company, 1973), pg. 502.

3. J. Wilson, *Lands of the Bible* (Edinburgh, 1847), iii. 284, quoted by Samuel J. Andrews, *The Life of our Lord Upon the Earth* (New York: Charles Scribner's Sons, 1891), p. 295.

I've been in some terrible storms, and I can still remember the pounding hail that shattered windows and battered cars. Nearly all those storms brought blinding sheets of rain driven by high winds that rocked skyscrapers and uprooted trees. Some of the most frightening storms even brought darkness in the middle of the day! I have to say that I've faced storms in my spiritual and emotional life that were far worse and even more deadly! I survived only because I hid myself in the Rock that was higher than I (Ps. 61:2)!

The storm that swept over those small boats on the Lake of Galilee had the fury and destructive power of a hurricane or typhoon! It came suddenly and without warning, and it just kept on coming without relief. The waves it created were so high that they swept over the decks, and the disciples were afraid they would sink the ships!

Where was Jesus during all of this excitement? Jesus was sound asleep. resting in His Father's perfect will. In fact, He was the Will of God! He had just finished an exhausting day of ministry to a clamoring crowd of people who wanted to physically drag Him to Jerusalem and crown Him as their earthly King. Then He spent some time explaining to His disciples all the parables He had given in His messages to the crowds. When the disciples sent the crowds away and they finally set sail for the other side of the lake, Jesus took advantage of the rare opportunity to get some rest.

I believe Jesus knew He would meet the demon-possessed man from the Gadarenes on the other side. As for the storm, Jesus must have known it would come too, but He didn't even bother to worry or think about it. He went to sleep because He knew that the storm was just an empty work of satan. There was nothing in the devil's arsenal that could stop or hinder Jesus because He was the Will of God in the flesh! If you and I can get to the place where we are so sold out to the purpose of God that we offer up our bodies as a living sacrifice to God, then we can also become the will of God encased in flesh! It takes total surrender and submission to the Holy Spirit.

The devil knew their destination, and he had something to protect. He didn't like to see his demons disturbed. Everywhere Jesus or His disciples went, his demons were being thrown out of people's hearts and trampled on. He was determined to keep those boats from getting to the other side, but he just didn't understand what he was coming against!

Jesus, the incarnate Will of God, had a divine appointment on the other side. There were people in need who had captured the attention of their heavenly Father, and they were about to have a life-changing encounter with the Son of God. He had an appointment to heal and deliver a crazed man from legions of demons. He had a 12-year-old girl to raise from the dead, and there was a desperate woman who was bleeding to death and in desperate need of His healing power. While the disciples were bailing water and fearing the worst, that woman was spending another pain-filled night in Decapolis thinking it might be her last!

The devil was saying to himself, "I refuse to let them get over there. I have too much to lose!" By the way, have you noticed how the devil was always messing with Jesus? Okay, then you need to quit acting so surprised and confused when he decides to mess with you too! The Bible clearly tells us:

The disciple is not above his master, nor the servant above his lord. It is enough for the disciple that he be as his master, and the servant as his lord. If they have called the master of the house Beelzebub, how much more shall they call them of his household? (Matthew 10:24-25).

God Is For You

I don't know why so many of us act like a storm is proof that the Lord doesn't really "love" us, or that something is obviously wrong with our lives! We start thinking, *Well, maybe I'm not fasting enough, maybe I'm not praying like I should, or maybe*

my confession isn't just right..." Listen, as long as you are doing your best to obey the will of God in your life, then you probably aren't guilty of any great sin or omission worthy of a
"Jonah storm," so don't get confused. Don't get frustrated and
run away from the Church. Don't condemn yourself over something silly and leave God and His Word. Stay with the Word of
God, *especially* in the middle of the storm.

Why am I saying this? It is the Word of God that teaches us,
"Yea, though I walk through the valley of the shadow of death,
I will fear no evil: for Thou art with me" (Ps. 23:4). Have you
forgotten that God is with you in the middle of your storm? That
is what the disciples did in the middle of the Lake of Galilee;
they forgot that the King of Glory was sleeping calmly in the
boat with them. They didn't realize that the lake they were on
was literally created and sustained by the living Incarnate Word
dozing in their boat! God can stop the very elements driving the
storm in your life because they only exist by His grace and
mercy! God is literally in the middle of your storm! And that
same God can stop the storm anytime He pleases! You are in the
hands of the Almighty Creator, and He is *for you*, not against
you. There are different kinds of storms, but in all of them, God
is supreme.

In the dark of night—when the storm seems to rage out
of control and threaten your life and every hope you have for
tomorrow—remember who you are and whom you serve! You
are on a divine mission that began at the moment you were con-
ceived! Your destiny is to fulfill the purpose of God in the earth,
and nothing but disobedience on your part can stop you! Death
has no power over you. Declare the unchanging Word of God to
the enemy of your soul: "Greater is He that is in me, than he that
is in the world" (1 Jn. 4:4b).

Have you taken the time to stop and realize that God is in
you? Even in the midst of the storm, God is in you! Declare it
out loud, "Even in the midst of this hurricane, dear God, I know

You are in me! Thank You, Jesus! Thank You, Lord!" Storms bring problems, but they do not have to bring defeat!

> *…and they awake Him, and say unto Him, Master, carest Thou not that we perish?* (Mark 4:38).

In this particular storm, the disciples faced two big problems that threatened to overwhelm them, and Jesus faced three big problems! The disciples were being beaten and threatened by the awesome force of an atmospheric disturbance and by a troubled lake. Jesus was confronted by both of these problems as well as by His fearful disciples who asked Him a question that demanded a quick response.

CHAPTER EIGHT

COMMANDING THE STORM!

God Is Right Where You Are

The enemy loves to get you in the middle of a storm and then ask you, "Who is this Jesus, anyway?" The devil waits until you think you are stranded in a swamped boat out in the middle of a hopeless storm, then he tells you, "If Jesus was with you…" or "If Jesus was really in your life…" The enemy will cause you to say to yourself, "Well, you know, when I got in the storm, it looked like God wasn't anywhere around."

The Russian cosmonauts said the same thing. When they orbited the earth, they said they couldn't find God in space. The problem wasn't with God, it was with their ability to perceive Him, for "God is a Spirit: and they that worship [or seek] Him must worship Him in spirit and in truth" (Jn. 4:24). Another problem is that "…he that cometh to God must believe that He is, and that He is a rewarder of them that diligently seek Him" (Heb. 11:6). It doesn't matter whether you face a storm in your marriage or in a space capsule hundreds of miles above the surface of the earth, He is there the entire time!

Jesus was right there with the disciples the entire time. When they got in the middle of the storm, their doubts overcame their faith. They found out their limited idea of who Jesus was didn't match the reality of their problem!

The disciples had seen Jesus work miracles right in front of their eyes, but they didn't really understand who He was. When they looked at Him sleeping in the stern of the boat. But they mistook His total peace and authority over the circumstances for total apathy about their problems and weakness in the face of the storm's fury!

When they said, "...carest Thou not that we perish?" (Mk. 4:38), they actually thought Jesus was going to die with them, and they were angry about Him not caring about it! To the Lord, it must have sounded like children who are crying to their parents, "Mom and Dad, don't you even care that we're starving?" In the same way that hungry child who complains to his parents really isn't "starving," the disciples weren't in danger of dying. They had been given to Jesus by His Father, so nothing and nobody had the power to snatch them out of His hand (see Jn. 10:28). Yet every time the water level in the boat got higher, so did their level of fear and panic.

God Has a Reason

As usual, fear produced a crop of doubtful questions and hidden accusations. Those water-logged disciples were probably glancing over at the sleeping form of Jesus and muttering, "What in the world are we doing on this ship, anyway? Why did He tell us, 'Let's go to the other side'?" I can almost hear John, Mark, and Matthew saying, "Man, if we are supposed to be going to the other side, and if He knew all along that this storm was coming, then how come He didn't...?!" That is exactly the way we talk, isn't it?

"Well Pastor Reems told us to fast Tuesday and Friday, and you know what? My storm is getting worse! I've had it. I'll tell you what I'm going to do—I'm going to get me something to eat!" Not to be outdone, another frustrated believer might add their thoughts about the situation: "Yeah, Pastor Reems told me to come to that early morning prayer meeting. Now I've gotta tell you that ever since I've been going to that prayer meeting at that ungodly hour, the enemy has been rocking my boat! He done all but tore it up! I tell you, I'm gonna quit going to that prayer thing."

The disciples didn't have any problem "walking the faith walk" once the tense moment with the prayer was over and they noticed bread miraculously multiplying as they passed it out to the big crowd that followed them. They didn't have any problem sticking with Jesus when He was healing blind people and teaching in the temple among the top religious leaders of Israel. They just hadn't counted on this underwater Bible class!

We face the same problems in the Church today! It seems as if half the people in a congregation will tune out the preacher if he's not "shakin' and quakin' " with a hot sermon punctuated with lots of ear-tickling phrases and eye-pleasing antics! "You know, I went to church and Pastor Reems didn't preach at all today, you know. She was just doing some of that old dry teachin', and she was jumping all over us with lots of Scriptures." Then someone else might chime in, "Honey, you need to go on the field with Pastor Reems. That's where she really preaches! If you ever want to hear Pastor Reems really preach, then go to Chicago with her. Man, she tears it up!"

Jesus had a reason for everything He did while He was on this earth. In the same way, most pastors have some pretty good reasons for most of the things they do. I know I have a very specific purpose for "tearing it up" in certain churches outside of my city. Very often, my responsibility in those situations is to "preach off their religious shoes." I literally preach until they kick their shoes off and enter into a new freedom of worship and surrender to God's Spirit.

In my own church, I operate under the mantle of a pastor, and I'm responsible for the consistent feeding and nurturing of my sheep. I can't feed them rich deserts all the time. They need the meat of God's Word, and they need the detailed exhortation and direction of a shepherd. It's not as glamorous, but it is necessary. Sometimes I want the sheep in my care to sit in their

seats instead of jumping up and shouting, because I know they
need to hear a sober word from God to help them with a very
specific problem or weakness.

God's in Control—Yesterday, Today, and Forever

Things haven't changed much. That day it was the disciples.
Today it is you and I—we're stuck in the middle of a storm trying to decide whether we are going to "backslide" or not! Listen
friend, this is not the time to backslide! I don't care what anyone
says, many times God puts you, or allows you to be, in a storm
to purify you!

Every time you and I survive a storm, our faith in God
grows and we graduate to another dimension in God's glory!
What do you think the Lord is trying to tell us in the verse that
says, "But we all, with open face beholding as in a glass the
glory of the Lord, are changed into the same image from glory
to glory, even as by the Spirit of the Lord" (2 Cor. 3:18).

God may have you in a storm because He is trying to get
your attention. He may have you in a storm so He can impress
His Word on you for a specific purpose or mission. He may be
saying through the noise and commotion of the wind and
waves, "I'm getting ready to use you. I'm getting ready to
anoint you. I'm getting ready to bless you. Fear not, it is I who
placed you in the middle of the storm, and it is I who shall deliver you!"

You don't have to pray and fast for 40 days to figure out that
God isn't out to destroy you! God isn't secretly scheming to get
rid of you. God loves you, and you need to tell yourself that day
by day. Just tell yourself, "*God loves me. God cares about me.
God knows about me, and He will never forget about me. God
has a plan for my life, and He will not allow it to fail!*"

On the other hand, people may look at you and think that
you are just wonderful, while God knows that you aren't. He
knows the real you. He knows if you don't have the faith that
you are always shouting about. He knows if you don't have the

joy that you claim to have when you run up and down those aisles of the church. Jesus was in the middle of that storm with Judas Iscariot, the disciple who would betray him, the treasurer who took money for himself out of their ministry expense account. Jesus was in the same boat with Thomas, who would be known from generation to generation for his doubting nature. He shared that boat with Peter, the first man to publicly recognize His deity and the disciple who would deny Him three times. Jesus knows if you are just trying to impress, suppress, or possess others. God says, "You don't have to impress Me. I know what is in you, and I am going to take you through the storm for your own good!"

The 12 disciples were very human men who were just like you and I! Every time God blesses us we get together and talk about it, but we have problems putting together the "big picture"! I can hear Peter saying, "Man, I never saw anything like that in my life! I saw it with my own eyes!" Then Thomas interrupts to say, "I wasn't there, so I really can't get excited about all this..." Brother Peter jumps right back in to say, "Well, I was there. I think He is the Son of God. I watched Him take those two fish and five loaves of bread. After He blessed them, He actually used them to feed all those people—thousands upon thousands of men, women, and children!"

But then the storm came. When you get in the middle of the storm, the enemy always tries to steal your faith and joy. He'll steal your blessing if you let him! In the middle of that storm old Peter forgot about the miracle of the wine at the wedding in Cana. He forgot about the time his mother-in-law was sick, and Jesus told her, "Get up off that bed and be made whole." Right now this same Peter was drenched and miserable. This great man of faith and power was asking Jesus, "Master, Master, carest Thou not that we perish? What are You doing sleeping? What's wrong with You? We're about to perish. We're about to die. Carest Thou not that we perish?"

In the middle of the storm, it is easy to forget that Jesus is in command. Even though the wind and the waves seem "out of control," they are firmly within the Master's grasp. Nothing is impossible for God. In fact, the word *impossible* has no place in a true believer's vocabulary. What appears impossible to us is well within God's reach. Commanding the storm would not be difficult for Jesus. No matter how disinterested He may have seemed to the disciples, Jesus was fully in control of the situation.

CHAPTER NINE

THE DELIVERER, THE PRINCE OF PEACE

God has power over every storm. Everything is not unto death. The enemy only presents us with a mirage of death. The Bible says that God lives in us. If God is in us, then we too have power over the storm. In the midst of the storm, God is in me. In the midst of the flood, God is in me. In the midst of the hurricane, God is in me.

Pray God's Will Into You

Because of satan's jealousy, envy, and hatred for God, he causes havoc and chaos in external things only to get you to question the power and presence of God. The enemy will put you in the middle of a storm; then he'll send lying demons to your mind and say, "God isn't with you." You should know that this is a lie because David already asked the question: Who can escape from the presence of the Lord? (see Ps. 139:3) God promised He would never leave us nor forsake us (Heb. 13:5).

Satan can only do what God allows Him to do. Even in the storm of Job, satan was only allowed to destroy all that Job owned, but he was forbidden by God to touch Job's life. Satan tampered with everything Job had in his attempt to get Job to curse God, but all it did was drive Job to worship God even more.

God does not intend for His people to walk around full of fear and anxiety. He intends for us to walk in power and love and have a sound mind (2 Tim. 1:7). Jesus could sleep and be at peace during the storm because He understood the purpose of God for His life. Jesus was in one accord with the Father. He even said that He did only what He saw His Father do (Jn. 5:19). I always encourage my church and all those that I come into contact with to develop a prayer life. Only prayer (communion with God) and the Word of God will sustain you in stormy weather. Only prayer will develop the will of God in you. When you become the manifested will of God then you can say like Jesus, "I only do what I see my Father do."

Jesus, unlike Jonah, walked in total obedience. Jesus, unlike Paul, walked in total deliverance from His own will. Many would say that only Jesus could walk in total deliverance. One thing that is often overlooked is that Jesus was a man of constant prayer. As long as He was in human flesh, He could have chosen to develop His own will, yet He chose to be delivered from Himself so that the will of God might be fulfilled through His life. This is why we can say that Jesus was the Will of God.

Shielded by Faith

Storms come on all fronts. While on that ship Jesus was in a three-dimensional storm. He was confronted by an atmospheric disturbance, troubled waters, and faith in conflict with fear. Hours before Jesus and His disciples departed on the ship, Jesus went into the mountains to pray. Jesus prayed alone. He went into the mountains in prayer and did what the Bible tells us to do in Ephesians chapter 6. Jesus put on the whole armor of God, and above all, He took the shield of faith. He was fully equipped for the journey across the water. The disciples, however, had not stopped to pray. They had failed to put on the armor of God.

Jesus could sleep on the ship because His shield of faith was raised high. The disciples were bothered by the howling wind, huge waves, darkened sky, and rain. They became full of fear, not faith. They asked doubt-filled questions among themselves. I can imagine them saying, "If Jesus is really who He says He is, He should have known that there was going to be a fierce storm today." Indeed, Jesus did know that there was going to be stormy weather. Jesus knew that while they were on the ship satan would send fiery darts of doubt and fear to pierce the shields of the disciples. The disciples had not taken time to oil their shields with prayer before going into spiritual battle. Without the daily application of oil, the leather on the shields lose its ability to absorb the onslaught of darts without breaking. Since the shields had not been kept in a state of preparedness through the oil of prayer, satan knew that all it would take for the disciples to doubt God was a little noise, wind, and water.

Many times God allows storms to come to purify you. He allows them to come so that He can take you to another dimension in Him. As with Job, He allows them to come to take you into a place of worship. He allows them to come to put His Word in you. He allows storms to come to prepare you. God allows storms to come to strengthen you.

In the middle of the storm, the enemy will come to steal your faith. The enemy will come to steal peace and joy. He will come to steal your blessing. Satan gets you so caught up with the wind and the waves that you forget who God is and what He has already done. Peter forgot about the man who had laid by the pool of Bethesda for 38 long years until Jesus told him to take up his bed and walk. Peter forgot about the wedding where Jesus turned the water into wine. Peter forgot about the feeding of the 5,000. The disciples forgot about all the miracles that Jesus had wrought in their presence. You can never allow the enemy to make you forget the testimony of who Jesus is to you.

I know Jesus as my healer. When I was dying of tuberculosis, Jesus stepped into my life. The doctor admitted that he couldn't help me, and then he said "You're going to die, Ernestine." Then my Lord stepped into the picture. He said, "Ernestine, you don't have to die. You can live because I am the Lord thy God, and I heal My people from all manner of sickness and disease. You are now made whole!" I don't know what kind of storm the enemy has released upon you, but I do know that Jesus can step into your storm and say, *"Peace, Peace be still"* (Mk. 4:39).

I give you Jesus! The epitome of deliverance. He is saying to you today, *"I am the will in the ship, in the storm, in the hurricane, in your sickness, in your affliction, in your financial dilemma. I am the Will of God."* The will of God is that all your needs be supplied. The will of God is that you walk in divine health. This is why some call Him *Jehovah Jireh*, Jesus provides; *Jehovah Nissi*, Jesus protects; *Jehovah Tsidkenu*, Jesus heals; and *Jehovah Shammah*, Jesus is right there. JESUS, JESUS, JESUS.

Peace in His Love

In the middle of the storm, God is saying, *"Peace, Peace; Jesus is aboard the ship."* Although it may seem as if He doesn't care, He does. Jesus is calm in stormy weather because He keeps His mind staid on God and therefore He is always in perfect peace (see Is. 26:3). Jesus is the will of God, and because He is the will of God, He can speak peace to stormy situations. When you get delivered from your own will and become the will of God even as Jesus, you can rebuke the wind, speak peace to the sea, restore faith to the fearful, and deliver those who are in bondage on the shore.

> *Master, carest Thou not that we perish? And He arose, and rebuked the wind, and said unto the sea, Peace, be still. And the wind ceased, and there was a great calm* (Mark 4:38b-39).

Frankly, we should never question whether the Lord loves us or not; because He sure puts up with a lot of garbage just to save and purify us! When the disciples woke Jesus from a sound sleep, the first words He heard from their mouths were words of accusation, anger, fear, and blame! They had seen Him work miracles again and again. They had watched and listened to

Him for weeks and months at a time, yet in the face of this storm, the disciples' first impulse was to point their fingers in blame. It isn't wise to accuse the Messiah, the sacrificed Lamb of God, of "not caring"! Jesus quickly rose in power and rebuked the wind and waves, perhaps so that His stern reproof of the disciples could be heard better!

And He said unto them, Why are ye so fearful? how is it that ye have no faith? And they feared exceedingly, and said one to another, What manner of man is this, that even the wind and the sea obey Him? (Mark 4:40-41).

Now I want to ask a question: And what manner of men are these, who, unlike the wind and the sea, refuse to obey and believe in Him? These two verses in the Gospel of Mark describe the greatest problem you and I will ever face in this life! We just can't grasp the fact that the God of the universe is on our side, and that He actually cares for us! In times of stress (which seems to be most of the time), we always seem to forget that the Lord is in our boat with us! We're so busy pointing our finger at Him or trying to "second-guess" His "motives" for putting us in a storm that we never consider His character, His loving promises, and His higher purpose in the Word. The Lord is with us— whether we're running like Jonah, obeying like Paul, or blindly bailing water and complaining like Peter and the other disciples! Jesus is the very will of God in our lives! He is in total command of every element and force we encounter! No wonder God's Word declares: "If God be for us, who can be against us" (Rom. 8:31b) The only variables He does not command are human beings like you and I, because He wants us to obey and seek Him by our own free will and conscious choice!

Jesus Can Do the Impossible to Deliver You

And they that did eat of the loaves were about five thousand men. And straightway He constrained His disciples to get into the ship, and to go to the other side before unto Bethsaida, while He sent away the people. And when He had sent them away, He departed into a mountain to pray. And when even was come, the ship was in the midst of the sea, and He alone on the land. And He saw them toiling in rowing; for the wind was contrary unto them: and about the fourth watch of the night He cometh unto them, walking upon the sea... (Mark 6:44-48).

The disciples were in serious boat trouble again. Those "contrary winds" that plagued the Lake of Galilee were at it again. According to Matthew's account, the disciples were being tossed around by high waves too (Mt. 14:24). They may have made it halfway across the lake before the storm hit and darkness fell. By the time Jesus walked across the water to them between three and six in the morning, they were still in the middle of a lake that only measures 13 miles long by 7 miles wide! They had literally spent the entire night rowing into the fierce wind without making any progress!

How many times have you felt stranded in the middle of your storm? The worst storms always seem to hit in the total darkness of the night, when you feel like you are all alone and helplessly adrift. Swept by the winds and buffeted by the waves of hostile elements, you are tempted to wonder if God is really there, and if He is, does He really care?

The disciples' situation was so serious that Jesus interrupted His prayer and time of mourning over the beheading and martyrdom of John the Baptist so He could go to the disciples' rescue! Did you notice that they didn't even have to pray or cry out to Him? The men were being obedient to obey His command to "go to the other side." He knew their need even from a distance and He quickly came to their rescue. Every time you find yourself in a storm because of your obedience to the Lord, you can rest in peace, knowing His watchful eye is upon you!

Their faith had grown, but they still limited the power of Jesus to a little theological box. They weren't prepared to see Him walk on water! And only one, Peter, dared to believe he could follow Jesus anywhere—even onto the surface of the raging Lake of Galilee (Mt. 14:28-31)!

God is saying to you in the middle of your storm, "Jesus is aboard your boat." You may think He is sleeping, or that He just doesn't care about the danger and fear you are battling. The truth is, He is not asleep. Trust me. He's not asleep. He knows what's going on. He knows everything about you. Jesus is the will of God in your storm. You need to quit letting the devil make you feel like you're not in God's will. You're in His will, and He is in you. He abides in you day and night. In fact, He has promised you: "I am with you alway, even unto the end of the world…" (Mt. 28:20). Let me tell you this: He is going to bring you out of your storm! God is going to bring you out even if He has to come to you in the middle of your storm! Your God isn't afraid to walk on water or do the impossible to protect His obedient sheep!

Sometimes you just have to stand still and see the salvation of God! Stop relying on your own strength, and stop blaming yourself when your own strength isn't enough! God isn't shocked; He's relieved that you have finally accepted the truth! Let God deliver you, and realize that only He can bring you out! Jesus said, "I am the way, the truth, and the life…" (Jn. 14:6). In Proverbs 18:10, the Bible says, "The name of the Lord is a strong tower: the righteous runneth into it, and is safe."

No matter how bleak your future looks right now, say to yourself, "I'm safe, because the Word of God declares it!" No matter how strongly the winds are trying to blows you off course, and no matter how high the waves may be, you are not alone! The God who made you, saved you, and called you knows exactly where you are and how you feel. He cares for you. Trust Him. The Bible says, "And My people shall dwell in a peaceable habitation, and in sure dwellings, and in quiet resting places" (Is. 32:18).

If the reality of it all hasn't hit you yet, I want you to understand the truth of this book today, because it can change your life like it did mine! Storms are going to come—no matter what you say, pray, do, or don't do! Get your rain gear together, and learn how to keep your eyes on Jesus in every storm. The rest is kind of up to Him. Storms will come, but your actions will determine what kind of storms will come into your life! That's right, you can be like Jonah, who tried to run from the will of God and ended up on a boat in the middle of a storm and then in the belly of a fish (I don't recommend this approach). You can also be like the apostle Paul, who was in the will of God in the storm. And believe it or not, you can be like Jesus, who was the will of God in the storm! Now that is a beautiful revelation!

Stay and See the Deliverance of the Lord

If you are like me, then at one time or another you have questioned God while you were bailing water in the middle of a dark storm. I finally had to accept the truth I found in God's Word: God uses storms to reprove us, cleanse us, wash us, and separate us. He allows storms to come into our lives. When He allows a storm to come, then quit squirming and don't try to run away from it. "For it is God which worketh in you both to will and to do of His good pleasure" (Phil. 2:13).

Just stay right there until you hear from God. He spoke to Brother Paul who was in the will of God in the middle of a storm, "Tell everybody if they stay in the ship, they will be safe." The ship was just a tool or temporary shelter—the real safety was in the covering and guidance of God through Paul. Only a few verses later, the men abandoned the ship as it broke up in the sea and they swam and floated to the Island of Malta— again in fulfillment of the Word of God through Paul. God is saying, "Just hold on. Just stay in My perfect will."

Don't let anybody rob you of your precious relationship with God. Don't let anybody or any circumstance make you give up the ship! God is going to bring you through it, and if you make up your mind to stand fast, then no power on earth can hold back your deliverance!

What shall we then say to these things? If God be for us, who can be against us? He that spared not His own Son, but delivered Him up for us all, how shall He not with Him also freely give us all things? Who shall lay any thing to the charge of God's elect? It is God that justifieth. Who is He that condemneth? It is Christ that died, yea rather, that is risen again, who is even at the right hand of God, who also maketh intercession for us. Who shall separate us from the love of Christ? shall tribulation, or distress, or persecution, or famine, or nakedness, or peril, or sword? As it is written, For thy sake we are killed all the day long; we are accounted as sheep for the slaughter. Nay, in all these things we are more than conquerors through Him that loved us. For I am persuaded, that neither death, nor life, nor angels, nor principalities, nor powers, nor things present, nor things to come, nor height, nor depth, nor any other creature, shall be able to separate us from the love of God, which is in Christ Jesus our Lord (Romans 8:31-39).

Some people claim that Paul didn't write the Book of Romans, and they may be right. But I'm telling you that whoever wrote that epistle sure knew what it meant to suffer! That man somehow knew a lot about the storms of life! Every kind of storm that you and I can face is listed in this passage of Romans! It is almost as if God knew we would need an encouraging word from somebody who has been in our shoes! Most of us avoid the kind of storms that old Jonah faced, but as long as we are breathing, we are going to be jumping on boats to "get to the other side" of the Lake of Galilee! It just comes with the territory of Christian discipleship.

Are you like Jonah? Are you trying to run away from God? Jesus is saying, "Come." I don't know about you, but He stepped into the middle of my storm and said, "Peace, peace, be still, be still." He's saying to you today, "I am the Will of God in your storm-tossed ship. I am the Will of God in the blustery storm winds blowing through you life. I am the Will of God comforting you and directing you in the hurricane of affliction. I am your financial deliverer. I am the Will of God, and My will is that you be supplied in all your needs. I'll supply them, I will heal you, I will save and deliver you. I will deliver, uplift, and bless you, for I am the same in the middle of your storm."

You Belong to Him

Be careful to stay in a place of submission and obedience so that when the storms arise in your life, you can say, "Peace, be still. All is well, for I am not my own, but I have been bought with a price! My life is not mine to command, for I belong to Another. It is He who establishes my steps, and He is with me this very moment—even in the middle of the storm! I declare by the Word of God that no weapon formed against me shall prosper!"

You can't stand up in a storm and declare, "Peace, be still!" when you're not in that holy place of obedience. We just don't know when a storm is going to rise up in our lives, our families, or our ministries. That is why I continually encourage my congregation to go to intercessory prayer meetings and Bible studies. I urge them to gather in His name every time the doors open. I don't do it out of legalism, I urge them to do it because I want them to have power when the storms arise! It is only through relationship, obedience, and communion with God that we will have the power to put a storm "in its place."

Know Your Savior

Both of the times the disciples were delivered from violent storms on the Lake of Galilee, they expressed shock and surprise when Jesus exploded their preconceived ideas about Him. Even God's Word can only offer us "snapshots," or limited facets, of the Lord's divine nature! "Who is He?" He is the Lily of my valley. He is my bright and Morning Star. He is the Joy of my salvation. He is the Lamb of God that taketh away the sin of the world. He is my rod, and my staff, who parted my Red Sea so I could escape from bondage and enter my promised land! He is my living veil in the Most Holy Place. He is joy unspeakable and full of glory. He is my "wheel in the middle of the wheel" (see Ezek. 1:16), and He is the Lover of my soul.

You may see Him as a hope for the hopeless, or He may be the mother that you lost when you were just a lonely, hurting little child. He protected you. He watched over you. He kept you. You may see Him as the Savior who stepped in when you lost your father at the age of two. He kept you then. He loves you, and He'll continue to keep you now.

The enemy will throw everything he can at you to make you leave your church and backslide. In the middle of the pain, can you hear the Holy Spirit saying, "Come"? The Holy Spirit is saying, "Come without money. Come without price." Jesus is saying, "Come." He loves you and He cares about you. God doesn't waste words or send messages to His people just to have them ignored. He speaks to us as children to bring correction, reproof, and edification to bless our lives. He wants to deliver us from the hand of the enemy and set us free! Then He will send us out to Nineveh, to Rome, and to the Gadarenes to bring salvation, deliverance, and wholeness to others. There will be storms along the way, but our God will deliver us out of them all!

"I'm saved. I love the Lord, but I'm in the storm." If you are in a storm, then you need to pray, "Lord, I'm deep in this storm, and I need to hear You say, 'Peace' to my storm." You or someone you know may be facing a storm of affliction, or a storm of doubt or fear. You might be suffering from the violence of a financial storm or a storm that is battering your marriage relationship. The Holy Spirit is ever present to deliver you. He is right there in the middle of the storm with everyone who calls upon the name of the Lord! He is there to bring freedom and victory.

"I don't understand why I am in this storm, but I know I need God." He's calling you because He cares for you. He is saying once again, "Peace, be still." In every area of your life, He's saying, "Peace, be still." Thank Him for it. It is time to receive God's blessings, deliverance, and salvation. "But as many as received Him, to them gave He power to become the sons of God..." (Jn. 1:12a). Victory in the storms of life doesn't come through begging and pleading. Victory in a storm doesn't have anything to do with feelings. It's not about what you feel, but what you believe. Thank you, Lord.

True salvation is deliverance from sin. Sin causes a yoke of bondage to be placed around your neck. Sin is laborious. This is why Jesus told us in Matthew 11:28-30:

> *Come unto Me, all ye that labour and are heavy laden, and I will give you rest. Take My yoke upon you, and learn of Me; for I am meek and lowly in heart: and ye shall find rest unto your souls. For My yoke is easy, and My burden is light.*

Respond to Him and Spread the News

Churches across America are loaded with people who have confessed Jesus Christ to be their Lord, but they have not surrendered their will to Him. Jonah was one of those people, one of those folks who possess a "holier than thou" attitude. Jonah served God as long as God's will did not meddle with his own ideologies. Jonah had a lot of religious ideologies, but in all of his religion, he was missing God.

I was afforded the opportunity to travel extensively during the Civil Rights era. I was a young woman from California traveling to Houston, Texas, to minister to the people there. I had heard a great deal about a beautiful, high-class department store there and wanted to see it while I was in town. When I went in that store, I experienced overt racism for the first time in my life. (This was about 35 or 40 years ago.) I went to a boutique in New Orleans and was told by the sales associate that I could not try on a hat until she asked her manager for permission because I was Black. I thank God every day for civil rights and nondiscrimination legislation. I no longer have to sit in the back of the bus. I no longer have to eat food handed to me out of the back door of restaurants. I can still remember reading signs that said, "Colored can't drink here." I never understood that type of persecution.

Civil rights afforded the extension of basic human rights to people of color. Civil rights blessed us, but even civil rights with all their benefits could not erase sin. Racism did not begin in the 1950's and 1960's. It was also prevalent in the days of old. Jonah did not want to preach to the people in Nineveh because they were not his people. They were not the sons and daughters of Abraham. Those people were heathens. Jonah disobeyed God. He rebelled against God and he went down. Many of us act like we don't understand why we keep going down. When you run from God, you have no other choice but to go down.

The majority of people in the church today will only witness or minister to their own kind—people who look, act, talk, and think like them. The Church is still segregated. We have Asian churches, Black churches, Caucasian churches, and Latino churches, etc. We fail to realize that there is but one Church. It is the Church of the Living God where there is neither Jew nor Gentile; bond nor free, male nor female (see Gal. 3:28). Everyone needs Jesus. He is the only one who can change situations. Jesus used His body to reach out to a lost and dying world. The real assignment of both Jonah and Paul was to tell a dying world about Jesus. God planned for Jonah to be His mouthpiece in Nineveh. God planned for Paul to be His mouthpiece in Rome. God used real people in the midst of trying circumstances (storms) to spread His message of deliverance.

God still uses real people today to take His message to a dying world. He still wants real people, like you and I, to tell the world about Jesus. You know that storm you just came through, the one that you thought was a hurricane force blowing through your life? Well, have you ever considered that God moves on mighty winds, sometimes winds strong enough to make us lose our grip on those tangible things so that we can grasp the intangible truths of His grace?

God uses storms to get us into position, the position where He can use us to fulfill His will. Too often we surround ourselves with positions that in the short-term appear to be advantageous, but have no real lasting effect. How many promotions did we seek in the working world, only to find less and less satisfaction with each raise or job promotion? How many positions of power have we sought in an effort to raise our self-esteem only to find emptiness and insecurity waiting at the top? The only position that is truly important is your *personal position* in relationship to God's will. Are you in alignment with His will today? Have you found the right position with God?

As you move through the storms of life, remember that fulfilling God's will occurs in the midst of the storms. If you see a storm brewing, do not run and hide. If God is in the midst of the storm, you cannot run from God anyway. Don't be like Brother Jonah, trying to hide below the deck. While you are busy hiding below the deck, God's outstretched hands are not within your view. God is always in position. We need to be in a position to receive His will.

God is always waiting, patiently—as the storm rages. He waits until we have positioned ourselves out in the open; battered, and torn, but not broken; poised to receive His blessings. Jonah, Paul, and Jesus experienced storms because God intended that these mighty men would be instruments of His will. Yes, even Jesus, though He was the Son of God, was an instrument through which God perfected His plan of salvation for the world. In the storm, you too can fulfill the will of God. Hold on to God through the storm, and use your "storms" to seek the will of God in your life. Glory and praise be to God in all things!

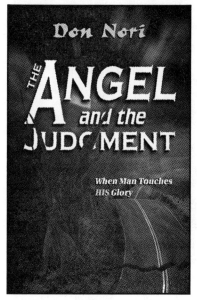

TELL ME AGAIN
by Dr. Patricia Morgan.
Tell Me Again is one woman's call to
hear the cry of the hurting, broken
children of the nations. An educational psychologist, a professor, and
a mother, Dr. Patricia Morgan com-
bines her culture, her beliefs, and her
passion to issue a ringing challenge
in this unique collection of writings.
This book will stir your heart like
nothing else can!
Hardbound, 144p.
ISBN 1-56043-174-1
(6¼" X 9¼") Retail $15.99

Available at your local Christian bookstore

IMAGE IS EVERYTHING
by Marvin Winans.
Yes, image IS everything! Does the
image God has of you match the
image you have of yourself? Society
today suffers many social ills because
of its lack of vision. Without an
image we aimlessly grope about in
life when we need to focus on what is
true and accurate. We need the image
that points us in the right direction—
because *Image Is Everything!*
Hardbound, 204p.
ISBN 1-56043-262-4
(6" X 9") Retail $17.99

Available at your local Christian bookstore

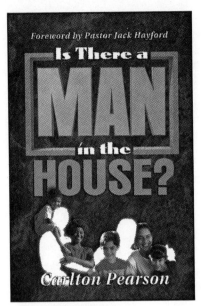